Reforming Welfare

GW00391186

Frank Field was appointed Minister for Welfare Reform on
2nd May 1997. He was elected to Parliament in 1979 as
the Member for Birkenhead.
Frank Field was previously director of the Child Poverty Action Group
and of the Low Pay Unit. A former Chairman of
the Social Security Select Committee, he is the author of
numerous works on welfare, low pay and social issues.

Reforming Welfare

FRANK FIELD

The Social Market Foundation
September 1997

This paper is dedicated to W.G.Runciman

First published by The Social Market Foundation, 1997
in association with Profile Books Ltd

The Social Market Foundation
11 Tufton Street
London SW1P 3QB

Profile Books Ltd
62 Queen Anne Street
London W1M 9LA

Printed in Great Britain by Biddles Ltd

A CIP catalogue record for this book is available from the British Library.

Paper NO. 32

ISBN 1 874097 917

Contents

Introduction

Frank Field, poverty and the Labour Party has never been a particularly easy or balanced equation. From the moment he first came to public attention in the late 1960s as director of the Child Poverty Action Group – producing the memo proclaiming that 'poor had got poorer' under Harold Wilson's first administration – Frank Field has never exactly fallen in with what the Labour Party of the day believed he should be thinking or saying.

That held true in the 1970s when he proposed – ahead of the Thatcher embrace of council house sales – that council housing should be transferred wholesale to its tenants to promote freedom and equality.

It remained equally true in the late 1980s and 1990s when Field turned himself from the opposition social security expert whom the Conservatives most feared into a self-appointed one-man think-tank charged with rethinking welfare from scratch.

On the way, much Labour had held dear in the past, including much that Field himself had at times accepted, has either been challenged or jettisoned – including Richard Titmuss' view that the causes of poverty and deprivation lie almost exclusively in economic and social structures, not in the character or behaviour of those affected.

The result for many traditional Labour supporters has been more than uncomfortable. Field's position accepts some of the analysis, though relatively little of the prescription, of Charles Murray and the political right – that benefits create dependency. He was the first serious Labour politician to characterise the social security budgets as 'out of control'. The first to restore the argument that benefit payments and their structures themselves affect behaviour. The first to maintain that benefit fraud should be a serious concern for Labour as well as Tory MPs.

Much of this has been conducted in language which stops in their tracks those with fixed ideas about where the political Left and Right lie – Field is happy to talk about 'an underclass'; to assault means-tests which are designed to target help for 'penalising effort, discouraging savings and taxing honesty'; to speak of 'cutting the supply routes' to young single parenthood and to demand that the social security system 'work with the grain of human nature'.

The result, however, has been Labour moving to meet Frank Field, not the other way around. And the revolutionary reformation of social security which he drew up while working as chairman of the Commons Social Security Committee has now been injected into the heart of government with his appointment as Minister of State for Welfare Reform.

As a result, this collection of speeches and essays is indispensable reading for anyone interested in the subject.

Frank Field's construction draws on many sources: Christian socialism; nineteenth-century ideas of self-help and the reconstruction of friendly society structures; a desire for renewed forms of the social insurance which under-pinned the post-war settlement; an acceptance that the limits of taxation have been reached for the present system and yet a firm conviction that a country reluctant to pay taxes must, nonetheless, find ways of spending more, not less, on welfare.

His grand design – 'a total reconstruction of welfare' in his words – runs, in places, with the tenor of the times which he himself has helped create: the desire, for example, to turn benefit offices into proactive agencies helping people back into a position where they can help themselves. In others, it runs against them: despite all the talk about stakeholding, for example, his wish to recreate mutual forms of saving and insurance comes just at the time when the existing mutuals, both building societies and banks, are moving in precisely the opposite direction.

Yet despite the complex nature of the origins of Field's programme, it has a degree of coherence which many other attempts to rethink welfare from the left have lacked. Its problem in part is that in the effort to square the circles it addresses, Field's proposition is a programme: money released from one part of the budget needs to be spent on another. And the immediate signs from the early months of the new Labour government have not all been encouraging.

His proposition, for example, involves the end of the State Earnings Related Pension Scheme when the government has just launched a review which has pledged to keep it. His favoured target for the £1 billion to be saved from introducing partial tuition fees for students is child care to enable more lone parents to go out to work. Instead the money looks set to go to the universities. The biggest version of Frank Field's 'big bang' involves switching half the cost of the NHS to an insurance tax. But there is no sign yet that the idea appeals to Gordon Brown, the chancellor. And the changes that Field advocates will also involve a significant extension of compulsory saving – an issue of which the government to date has fought shy.

Nonetheless, these are the ideas which Frank Field has brought into government and which Tony Blair put him in office, with a unique title, to develop. These essays set out the source and logic of Frank Field's thinking, the measures he advocates and the challenges to be overcome to realise them. They should be read.

Nicholas Timmins
September 1997

1: Strategies for Reforming the Welfare State

Speech to the Social Market Foundation/Manhattan Institute,

Conference on The End of Welfare, May 20th 1997

I want to outline the contours, as I see them, of the welfare debate unfolding in the country over the medium and longer term. There are, I think, three parts to the debate. The first is the framework of events and ideas. The second is the first principles from which I will be working and about which I am thinking. The final and main part is about strategies to counter dependency and low income.

First, the framework of ideas. One can polarise crudely the debate over welfare reform in this country and elsewhere, between two views. The first says you can explain the increase in the numbers of people on benefit by what has been happening in the wider economy both nationally and globally. The second says the rise in dependency – noticeable in this country and in others, particularly America – is to do with human motivation, the sorts of people who are on welfare and deep issues about their character. I think that both views offer partial explanations for the numbers of people on the welfare rolls in Britain today.

I would be presenting a very incomplete picture if I ignored what has been happening in the wider society over, let us say, the last fifteen or twenty years, not to trying to make a political point out of it. But it is important to bear in mind that since 1979 one third of all manufacturing jobs in this country has been wiped out. Overwhelmingly these were jobs which employed males. While some people might dispute the adequacy of the wages these jobs paid, they were the bedrock on which couples built their families and set about raising and nurturing children.

Of course if we look at the crude employment totals we see that there has been a large increase in the numbers of jobs after that first massive haemorrhage in manufacturing. But the composition of those jobs is different from those they replaced and it is the nature of many of these new jobs which helps to explain the inequalities in the distribution of work, which is now more marked than it was, say, twenty years ago.

Some people lay great stress on changes in the distribution of personal income. I put equal, if not greater, weight on the distribution of household income, and I am concerned about the unequal access to new jobs when they are created. I am concerned about the pay levels of those jobs and how they interact with the benefit system. It may go a long way to explaining why we have a growth of households where nobody works, and households where there may be two, three, four or more wage packets coming in. These economic changes are hugely significant in their impact on some families' well-being.

But there is also a second factor, the impact that the provision of welfare has on how people behave. I have always found it strange that so many people who get excited about the dangers of smoking and how important it is to stop people smoking, at the same time believe that you can spend £100 billion on welfare without influencing people's behaviour at all. I believe it does affect people's behaviour. How it affects it is the relevant question to ask. The task of the new Labour government is to understand rather than to condemn. The situation we find ourselves in is not generally man-made but the product of actions by successive governments. I am not in the business of blaming the victims when we, as politicians, should be looking much more seriously at our part in bringing about a tax and benefit system which has done so much to work against the verities we wish to see advanced.

The third aspect of the framework agenda is a belief about the reaction of taxpayers to all this. It links into what I want to talk about in terms of strategies. To use those words memorably applied to the imminent death of George v, the age of the quiescent taxpayer is peacefully drawing towards its close. The time when we, as politicians, can happily put our hands into taxpayers' pockets and draw out what we will is passing.

I do not want anyone to have the impression that we think that taxpayers will finance all that we wish to do. Indeed our mandate extends from accepting and being elected on a very clear platform of financial restraint. It means that the Department of Social Security – and I am sure other departments too – are having to think much more carefully about how budgets are spent, what our objectives are and how those objectives can be fulfilled using existing resources.

As far as the first principles within the framework are concerned, there seem to be four fundamental questions which we need to answer:

- What is the nature of welfare, what constitutes it and how should we define it?
- What underpins that provision?
- What values should welfare be teaching and what values should it not be teaching?
- How can welfare once again become an engine force for

social advance and betterment?

These questions ought to give more than a clue about what I see as one of the most important roles of government: to understand those forces and institutions in our society which advance the condition of the people and their social well-being. We look to government to foster and nurture those institutions, rather than cripple and destroy them.

The last area I want to address is the strategies for advance. I say 'strategies' in the plural, not in the singular. There is no one magic wand, or witch doctor's set of clothes in which we can dress ourselves, dance around and think something will happen. There are five strategies that I see. The first is to rebuild mass support for welfare in the country. That is why the first principal question I posed earlier about the nature of welfare will be so important. It also highlights a change of emphasis for the centre left. If you look at the success of Mr Attlee in building support for the welfare state, it was based on the fact that the poor and the working class were as often as not interchangeable terms in those days. Nobody had any doubts that his policies were about underpinning the living standards of the vast majority of people in this country.

Over time the emphasis of the welfare state began to change. Its widespread appeal began to shrink, people no longer naturally associated themselves with the welfare state because people, like in a previous incarnation, began to see welfare as that which only or mainly concerned the poor. I want to remove welfare from that ghetto and to rebuild its broad based support.

Second, we want to cut the supply routes into long-term dependency and the descent into hopelessness for those who are already there. David Blunkett, the Education Secretary, has already set about this by trying to raise the standards and achievements of individual pupils and to combat failure in individual schools which can have such an impact on children. Among young people there are two very vulnerable groups. Those young men who in times past would have expected to leave school with minimal skills but who would have achieved a reasonable job with reasonable rewards in the manufacturing sector which is now much shrunk. If people graduate from school now without possessing the most basic numeracy and literacy, or IT and social skills, they risk slipping into long-term dependency.

The other vulnerable group are young girls who go on to be young mothers. We know from the National Child Development Study who these people are likely to be. They are those girls who feel they never achieved at school – whether it is at primary or secondary school – but also those girls who are successes at junior school, but who fail to sustain that success in secondary school. Overwhelmingly very young mothers come from these two groups. Raising performance and achievement in our schools, then, is not only about recognising the importance and sacredness of every individual, but also about more mundane reasons – to stop people being recruited into long-term dependency on welfare.

Our third strategy is for managing the reform programme itself. If we are to copy anyone, I hope it will be the Lloyd

George model. The government must have confidence about the direction in which we believe we should head, but we must match that with the humility to learn about how our goals can best be achieved. We will be laying down our general principles and having as wide a debate as possible, both with our colleagues in parliament, with interested parties and, above all, with the country itself. In that way the reform programmes will be much more effective than they would be if we worked them out in private and then launched them on an unsuspecting public.

The fourth aim is easier to articulate than to achieve. But it is important to spell it out from the beginning so that we can be held to account on it. That is to move from a system which large numbers of people see as one of forced dependency to a system based on opportunity. As one single mother explained to me, having read about our various proposals she was so pleased we were going to move from a welfare state which gave a hand-up rather than a put-down. She felt that in the past she was always trying to take the initiative herself, but that she would be put down by the rules, the regulations, the officials and the law. Of course it will be difficult to make the transition from dependency to opportunity, but it is a very important objective.

The last strategy concerns the mechanisms of social advance. It is a personal testimony about how I see the role of government. That there is a role for government in all this is obvious, but it is not the one which has been classified so crudely as being either a top-down or a bottom-up approach. I hope you will see a government which uses its authority to establish a framework, but one which encourages innovation on the ground. We are looking for institutional reform which directly benefits particular groups, but which is also part of a much wider transformation which represents social advance and social betterment.

To summarise briefly, I spoke about the rudimentary framework which we are establishing for welfare reform. It is clear that there are economic factors which account for the rise in welfare dependency here and elsewhere. There is also the interaction between how the welfare system now operates and its effect on behaviour, what I would call 'character'. Finally there is the cautionary side to the debate: that we are ceasing to live in a society where taxpayers let us put our hands in their pockets and take out more money.

The question is, given the size of the government budget, how do we use what we have much more effectively? Delivery of welfare will be determined by what we see as its nature and how we redefine that as we approach the millennium. It will also be determined by an approach which views welfare not as something neutral but as a means of social advance and social betterment. We have to decide what values welfare should teach and what values it should not.

Finally, I said there were strategies. They are:

- the need to rebuild the coalition of support which used to exist for welfare – this will be determined in part by how successfully we answer the question about the nature of welfare
- the desire both to help people from dependency into

opportunity, and to stop them reaching dependency in the first place

- the requirement of putting our initial ideas before the country for debate, in a manner reminiscent of Lloyd George, rather than finalising the ideas in private
- the requirement that our reforms be rooted firmly in society rather than imposed on it and that we appeal to those organisations, and collections of individuals, who, by furthering their own interests, can promote the common good as well.

2: Self-interest and Collective Welfare: the Debate with Alan Deacon

Written in May 1997, during the general election campaign,
and revised after receiving Alan Deacon's comments

Alan Deacon leads the British academic debate on the changing philosophy of Britain's welfare. Part of his continuing contribution to this discussion has been the editing of a series of essays entitled *Stakeholder Welfare* [1] where contributors considered the ideas underpinning two of my recent publications: *Making Welfare Work* [2] and *How to Pay for the Future*.[3] More recently at a symposium held at Edinburgh University on 'The Future of Welfare', he presented a paper, *Self-interest and Collective Welfare: Frank Field and the debate about the future of welfare*. This is a response to the issues Deacon raises in his contribution to the Edinburgh symposium.

One of Deacon's concerns is to place the current welfare debate on a wider stage so that it is seen in the light of the main themes of the emerging political debate. He does this by combining the frameworks David Marquand and Lord Plant put forward in their essays in *The Ideas That Shape Post-War Britain*.[4] To this he adds a third dimension of his own.

Which Self?

In his essay 'Moralists and Hedonists', David Marquand attempts to break away from the simple nineteenth-century intellectual division between individualism and collectivism. Marquand offers 'the more subtle distinction between two conceptions of Self, of the good life and of human possibilities and purposes'. From the stance of a hedonist, Marquand sees 'Self' as composed of a static bundle of preferences with the good life being defined as one in which individuals pursue their own objectives without interference from others. In counter position are those who see Self as a growing moral entity and who consequently define the good life as Self seeking to adapt to higher preferences. [5]

Using this framework Marquand classifies political ideas and events in the British post-war period as passing through a number of distinct phases. According to Marquand:

- From the mid-1940s to the mid-1950s, the post-war generation of Keynesians exercised a collective, active and moralistic leadership.
- From the mid-1950s, and gathering pace during the 1960s, Keynesian Social Democrats abandoned what became seen as the patronising and strict moral activism of the Attlee government. Its place was filled by the values of the hedonist collectivists. Private pleasure was to be sought as a goal but within a public philosophy which elevated equality above all other values.
- By the mid-1970s this ethic was itself under attack from the New Right. Market systems were best, not just because the market was more efficient, but because here freedom could be exercised and only free people can be moral agents. Promoting what the nineteenth century saw as the 'vigorous virtues' was once again in vogue.
- This era was itself quickly challenged. Vigorous virtues need to be checked by a whole range of moral values, themselves inherited from a pre-capitalistic age. However, no such vibrant framework operated as an effective countercheck.
- Just as the hedonist collectivist ascendancy of the 1960s was routed by the moral certainties of Thatcherite individualism, so this period is itself now under challenge

from a new kind of moral collectivism.

Top-down or bottom-up?

To this framework Deacon adds a second dimension taken from another essay which runs alongside Marquand's. Lord Plant, drawing on the seminal work of Peter Clarke, *Liberals and Social Democrats*,[6] emphasises the distinction between top-down and bottom-up reformers.[7] Top-down reformers are classified as mechanical and bottom-up as moral. Plant explains the difference between the two approaches to political change as follows:

> Moral reformers are essentially bottom-up reformers. Values can only be effective in politics when they are widely shared and the task of the moral reformer is to take the long view and try to transform the values by which people live and the direction that he wants to see. The mechanical reformer is a top-down reformer who believes that there might [be] political, social and economic strategies available which would produce the desired results, without necessarily having to transform the underlying moral culture of citizens.[8]

Lord Plant is concerned to understand why the ideas, of which Tony Crosland was the chief advocate, collapsed so quickly with the first counter-offensive from Mrs Thatcher and her cohorts. The chief reason, according to Plant, is that Crosland was a mechanical reformer:

> The cost of mechanical reform . . . can be very high . . . if

one attempts to pursue a political strategy that does not draw deeply on the values held by the population at large, it may well collapse very quickly once it has been challenged by a belief system which is more confident about its salience to the main values of the society in which the reform is sought. It is really quite amazing that a political settlement so influenced by social democracy could have collapsed as quickly and as comprehensively as it did after 1979, and one of the explanations of this may well be that it was a form of mechanical or indirect politics. [9]

Traditional redistribution

To this framework a third dimension is added by Deacon himself. He questions the simplicity of the basic division in post-war politics between moralists and hedonists, or between top-down and bottom-up reformers. For him the crucial distinction lies between egalitarianism and anti-egalitarianism. What relevance has this three-dimensional framework to the approach I have taken to welfare reform which I proposed in the three volumes cited earlier?

A brief summary of my own position is called for here. The main beliefs underpinning the welfare reforms I have proposed are:

- The social security budget is not only by far the largest government programme, but its growth is progressively destabilising public finances. The social security budget is, coincidentally, also larger than any in the private sector.

- Self-interest is the most powerful motivating force in each of us. The denial of this basic force and the substitution of altruism have undermined welfare's appeal on two fronts. First, if a universal system is to prevail, welfare has to appeal to the majority. Altruism suggests a concentration of attention on other people rather than ourselves. Second, concentrating on the poor – all too often by way of means-tests – results in an undermining of civic society. Means-tests attack work, savings and honesty thereby adding to long-term dependency. A selective policy towards the poor, therefore, far from limiting the welfare budget, is one reason for its explosion.

- The age of the passive taxpayer is coming to an end. As more individuals are able to decide which goods and services define the good life, expenditure decisions become part of, rather than simply a means to, that end. The current debate will consequently move on from its preoccupation with resisting tax increases to one which demands major tax cuts.

- Yet more, not less money needs to be spent on welfare. This particular circle can be squared only by offering a stakeholder status where individuals contribute to their own individual accounts.

- A fundamental element of this new scheme is the consideration of how the poor can be accorded equal status. Will the stakeholder approach be backed with such enthusiasm that taxpayers willingly make contributions for the least well-off?

- That possibility will be enhanced if such payments are

17

made conditional on behaviour which taxpayers want to
see rewarded.

Do these ideas fit?

Where does Deacon place within this framework the ideas I
have developed for the reform of welfare? In his paper, *Self-
interest and Collective Welfare*, he writes:

> Strictly speaking, Field is neither a moralist nor a
> mechanical reformer in [the] terms [described by Plant]
> because he argues explicitly against a policy of
> redistribution *per se*. Furthermore, he is seeking neither
> to transform the values by which people live nor to by-
> pass the values through an indirect strategy as that
> applied by Crosslandite social democracy. What Field is
> offering is a more honest version of mechanical reform:
> one which accepts the centrality of self-interest to the
> electorate but which tries to channel the pursuit of that
> self-interest so as to produce a desired outcome.

Indeed, he suggests I am trying to achieve two objectives:

> First, to reform welfare so as to ensure that the majority
> who are not poor make provision for the contingencies
> of old-age and illness which is more adequate than that
> which they presently secure through the state. Second, to
> lessen the marginalisation of the poor by making their
> inclusion worthwhile to those who will have to pay for
> it. The attainment of the second objective is the more
> difficult, but the attainment of the first requires that a

clear distinction be maintained between what the majority pay for their own 'stake' and that which they pay on behalf of those who would otherwise be excluded from contributory insurance. There is no guarantee that such an approach will succeed, but considerable evidence that the alternative strategy failed.[10]

Limits to politics

The strategy to achieve the inclusion of the poor is correctly stated by Deacon. If social security is to prosper it has first to cater for the needs of the majority who must see an interest in its continuation and development. People worried about their own, their parents' and their children's future are unlikely to concentrate their attention on the least well-off. The poor can only be protected by schemes which the better-off majority want to see prosper.

However, the ideas I have put forward do not sit easily with any of the three-fold framework Deacon has put together. The ideas in *Making Welfare Work* and the subsequent two volumes are, if I accept Lord Plant's model of how best to seek radical reform, a combination of top-down and bottom-up strategies. But, in respect of the bottom-up approach I see a much more limited scope for effective action than appears to be suggested in Plant's framework. *Making Welfare Work* proposes using the legislative route to set out a new welfare framework (i.e. top-down), but the aim of that legislation is to bring about a fundamental change in how individuals operate (i.e. bottom-up). But it would be wrong to cast this aspect of a bottom-up approach as a moral one, as defined by Plant. It is not a question of seeking the means by which the values of individuals are changed. It is rather a question of setting a legal framework where natural decent instincts guided by self-interest are allowed to operate in a manner which enhances the public good. Hence the onslaught on means-tests in the reform programme I have put forward. Means-tests corrupt our natural decent self-instincts. Set the right framework – i.e. a welfare system which accepts as its starting point that individuals wish to better themselves and their families, and allows them to do so – and 'the moral improvement' (I would prefer to describe this change as an increase in social well-being) will take place.

As my approach differs quite significantly from that described by Lord Plant perhaps I should re-emphasise what I have just said. The politics I advocate are in sympathy with Lord Plant in so far as they reject the simple top-down approach to political activity. I have never believed that such a strategy could deliver political success in the longer run.[11]

For ideas to flourish over the longer run they have to be in tune with current aspirations and moods. Politicians can only buck the political market for a short period of time. But a new legislative framework, i.e. a top-down approach, can assist or constrain the flourishing of desirable values. The civilised values which most politicians wish to see cultivated are produced over centuries. Democratic politicians can do very little politically, in the short run, to change them. What they can do is to stunt their natural flowering. Right political activity is about supporting at every opportunity the age-old verities of civic responsibility at the expense of the darker side of human nature, i.e. to provide an environment where those values crucial to a civilised society can flourish.

New form of collectivism

Do the ideas in *Making Welfare Work, How to Pay for the Future* and *Stakeholder Welfare* fit easily into the new kind of collectivism which Marquand now sees as beginning to dominate the political arena? As with all Marquand's work, the reader has the excitement of participating in a journey of ideas, and of being presented with an original narrative knitting together such ideas and events. But Marquand himself questions the subtlety of his own classification: 'my stylised account is, by definition, incomplete and over simplified'.[12]

Certainly Marquand's fifth category of ideas into which he sees Britain moving is all too briefly stated. His total explanation runs to only a few lines:

> so the hedonist individualism of late-Thatcherism is now
> under attack from what looks suspiciously like a new
> kind of moral collectivism. Moral-activitist drumbeats are
> sounding once again. The drummers are collectivists, not
> individualists.[13]

Do the welfare reforms I advocate resonate with the drumbeat of a new form of moral collectivism? The word 'moral' provokes a negative reaction from me in much the same way as my use of the term 'character' upsets Alan Deacon.[14] While Noel Annan initiated a new appreciation of the impact of evangelicalism in British life [15], subsequently and substantially added to by Boyd Hilton, evangelicalism still has a mixed result sheet. The transformation of England into the nation of the book, with the Bible playing the same role as the Koran in the Muslim world today, and the attempt of good works to humanise the face of early capitalism, needs to be valued positively in any consideration of the impact of evangelicalism on Victorian society. But so too does its far less attractive side. The evangelical legacy of an unhealthy prurience of a self-righteous and largely self-appointed corps poking its sticky fingers into the private lives of individuals has, for me, an inescapable association with the use of 'moral' when it is applied in public debate. Hence my use of the word 'character'. I attach great significance to how each of us goes about our daily business. And I see life in terms of individuals seeking not simply to achieve their full potential – to use a current cliché – but in the Idealistic terms which are hinted at in the second of the two primary categories about the Self with which Marquand begins his essay, and which is developed so sensitively by Lord Plant and his colleague.[16]

But if collectivism is to be seen exclusively in terms of equality, achieved by an increase in public expenditure on public services – for that is how Marquand appears to be using the term in his essay – the ideas I have put forward cannot be squared with what he sees as a revival of his essentially Croslandite philosophy.

But nor do I seek merely to increase the size and importance of private welfare. While stakeholder welfare attempts to entice the richer citizens to pay more for their own welfare, the issue is not one of more private arrangements. The objective is rather to offer individual ownership *within* a collective provision. I advocate, I believe, a sense of equality which Tawney would have recognised. I see citizenship partly in terms of doing things in common. Hence the importance of universal stakeholder status.

Because much of what I have written argues against an extension of the State Earnings Related Pension Scheme (SERPS), it is assumed to be an advocating in its place an extension of private pension provision. This is not so. But nor do I wish to wage a war on the private sector; my objective is different. It is to nurture forms of collective provision which are independent of the state. On one plane, this third way presents the reformer with a bed of political nails. It entails a form of political conduct which has largely ceased to be practiced – at least on a national scale. Merely to propose how a mutual aid model can succeed, when success depends partly on an army of individuals organising responsibility within a multiplicity of guilds and societies, hints at the political mountain to be climbed. The temptation for politicians to opt either for a state scheme, or to encourage the private sector to advance, is obvious – but it is a temptation which I believe should and can be resisted. And there is, as I suggest, an alternative.

First, I will explain the role I see for redistribution, for it plays an important part in the reforms I propose – but the means and objectives are different from Crosland's. Deacon underscores the extent of redistribution in what I have proposed and here two comments are relevant. First, Deacon concentrates attention on additional redistribution over and above that already achieved. I am interested in defending the extent of redistribution which currently takes place in our welfare arrangements, partly because it benefits most those on the lowest earnings, but also because it helps build a sense of shared endeavour and common interests.

The current welfare scheme does deliver important and significant redistribution towards the poorest people. Over a third of the total welfare bill goes on the payment of the state retirement pension. Generally speaking richer people live longer than poorer people, and so draw a pension for many more years. The poorest also have the most chequered employment record and the system of credits for periods out of the labour market is an important redistributory element, especially for those who have long periods away from the work-place as mothers or carers for elderly relatives. Moreover, these pensions form a much higher proportion of the total income of poorer pensioners.[17]

Second, as Deacon rightly underlines, for stakeholder welfare to function in the way I envisage, a significant element of redistribution is involved. But I have failed to convince him of the extent of redistribution called for if stakeholding is to become an inclusive rather than an exclusive political movement. Those outside the labour market require their contributions (not credits) to be paid and those in low paid work similarly require assistance. This redistribution will only be forthcoming if two criteria are met. The first is that the stakeholder approach is enthusiastically backed by the electorate at large. The second is that, even with the necessary backing from the electorate, this new aspect of redistribution will be conditional. Taxpayers are likely to stump up a contribution for poorer stakeholders only if they approve of the behaviour of those for whom they are contributing.

How we begin introducing the extension of redistribution is crucial to its outcome. We need to start with those groups who command the greatest public sympathy. That is why I suggested in *How to Pay for the Future* that the first group to incorporate into the stakeholder status were carers. Not only are they a clearly defined group for benefit purposes, they are also in receipt of the invalid care allowance, but their role is one which is warmly and widely approved.[18] Before incorporating other groups, the government will be required to satisfy taxpayers that the claimants are genuine, e.g. that the long-term sick and disabled are just that. This is far from the true status of all claimants at the moment. Hence the need for effective counter-fraud strategies. This move is a prerequisite for delivering the stake for non-earners in stakeholding welfare. Yet even when the claimant files have been secured, the size of the groups who will qualify for an enhancement of their stakeholder pension will be considerable. So therefore will be the bill for including them.

This discussion leaves three major issues largely untouched, two of which were raised in Deacon's paper. These issues are:

- How can social advance best be achieved and how does this relate to the kinds of political activity described by Plant?
- Is the issue of character helpful to the evolving welfare debate?
- What is the balance between altruism and self-interest,

and in striking a new balance have I exaggerated
differences between my ideas and post-war orthodoxy?

I will look at each of these in turn.

How best to achieve social advance

Implicit throughout *Making Welfare Work* and *How to Pay for
the Future*, is a belief about the proper role for politics in
human affairs. Deacon rightly emphasises that my starting
point is human nature, its fallen status, and the centrality I
accord to self-interest. One of my main criticisms of current
welfare is that a massive labyrinth of rules, regulations and
entitlements more often than not attempts to govern self-
interest in an unnatural, and thereby futile manner. When the
right ordering of human nature is pitted against welfare,
human nature will invariably win. Hence the current *status
quo* where the penalties against work, savings and honesty are
so harsh that fraud or dependency are ubiquitous. But these
criticisms of the outcome of current welfare arrangements,
while important, are the negative side of the positive strategy
which is my primary concern. This is to try and understand
the means by which societies advance and to nurture such
means of advance and greater well-being. This, I believe, is
the primary duty of politicians. Their actions are secondary,
although of importance. Political actions implement reforms
which either help or hinder the natural instincts among
voters in seeking the means of social advance.

In the years preceding the turn of the century, reformers
who saw themselves as on both the Left and the Right of
British politics sought first to understand the transformation

in the position of skilled and semi-skilled families in Britain.[19] They believed that the friendly society and mutual aid movements had located an engine force of social change which was as widely admired and applauded as it was effective in transforming living standards. It was in the replacement of these self-governing guilds and societies by top-down state provision that much of today's welfare ills are to be found. My criticism of both the Lloyd George reforms, and those proposed by Beveridge, is that they struck at the motive force of social advance. The emphasis of the reforms I propose are essentially about strengthening existing mechanisms for social advance and therefore social well-being.

Character and behaviour

Deacon sees my contribution as explicitly setting out to highlight the impact of welfare on behaviour. It most certainly attempts to do that. Further, Deacon writes that I 'have tackled head on a series of difficult issues which many commentators on the Left have been reluctant to acknowledge as legitimate matters of debate'.[20] To me this is a central concern and not a mere vacuum to be filled. It is at the very centre of where the welfare debate needs to be. To help explain why I believe this is so, let me move to the use of the words 'character' and 'behaviour'.

Alan Deacon is concerned at the way I use both of these terms, believing I use them imprecisely and interchangeably. Deacon's aversion to the term 'character' stems largely from the way the term has been historically deployed. He also quotes James Q. Wilson who argues that some people will not respond in an expected manner because they do not have the same values, beliefs and habits as everyone else. In Wilson's words, 'To put it plainly, they lack character'.[21] Moreover, this lack of character calls for sanctions.

I do not for a moment believe that sanctions are not sometimes required. But for politicians to strut around in a macho fashion calling for tougher and tougher sanctions against the poor completely misreads the scene as I see it. There are indeed feckless and idle claimants. It would be amazing if the poor were exempt from the social parasites which exist in all other social groups. The thrust of my argument is that a major consequence of welfare is now the cultivation of idleness, fecklessness and dishonesty. I do not condemn the poor for responding rationally to the welfare framework which politicians impose upon them, although I am unhappy about it. Apart from seeking to support and salute the majority of claimants who behave honourably, despite all the incentives to do otherwise, my energies go towards seeking reforms which will encourage the natural positive instincts in all of us – as present in the poor as any other group – to flourish.

This aspect of my response to Alan Deacon needs to be read in conjunction with two other recent papers of mine, *Welfare: New Labour Markets and Fiscal Reform* (Chapter 4)[22] and *Rebuilding Mutual Aid* (Chapter 5)[23]. Merely changing the welfare framework is insufficient. The reforms for single mothers I advocate will lead to a mass exodus into part-time work which is declared, and then for a large number of single mothers to leave the welfare roles completely. A new norm of working single mothers will be established – which is what most of them wish to do anyway, and which a sizeable minority already achieves. Peer group pressure will then operate helping to reinforce the new norm. That some single mothers may still refuse to behave in a responsible way will then have to be faced. But to assume that all or most will react in such a way, even when offered alternative opportunities, is a travesty of what will happen. This belief does not, in any way, lessen the need to cut the supply route to single parenthood. In Chapter 4 I suggest how this operation should be staged.

In his response to this section, Deacon justifiably pushes his point on the need to make a clear distinction between 'character' and 'behaviour':

> You explain that you do not blame the poor for responding rationally to the incentives presented by the welfare system, and suggest that if the system were reformed in ways which would encourage the 'natural positive instinct in all of us', the poor would respond. The article by Wilson, however, argues the opposite. For Wilson the poor are poor *because* they lack character, they do not share these instincts, they will *not respond* to any set of incentives because their 'psychological muscles' are corrupted. That is why strategies aimed at improving incentives will always fail and only sanctions will work. That is why *he* is talking about *character* and *you* are talking about *behaviour*.[24]

He concludes, not unfairly, 'I rest my case'. I would merely add that welfare conditions behaviour that changes in welfare can transform behaviour and that different behaviour can bring forth different character traits.

Attack on post-war orthodoxy

This leads the discussion on to the final topic on which I wish to comment. Deacon writes that I overstate the differences between myself and post-war orthodoxy [25]. Later in his paper he observes, 'It is universally acknowledged that Titmuss' ideas dominated academic discussion of social policy for most of the post-war period'.[26] But Titmuss did not only dominate the academic debate. He was also a pervasive influence in the political world of social policy. Deacon writes that 'in his commitment to equality and social integration Titmuss was the spiritual heir of Tawney'.[27]

Here Deacon is less robust than he normally is in evaluating Titmuss' work. The Titmuss world was, however, built on sand. As in other essays, Deacon cites the work of Simon Robinson which stresses the Christian conception of human nature which was central to Tawney's politics. Titmuss held a view totally at variance with Tawney's stance – the fallen side of mankind was written out of his script.

While Deacon has pointed this out on a number of occasions, he has failed, I believe, in *Self-interest and Collective Welfare*, to draw out its significance. This is not a mere quibble. No one set of reforms built on such a false reading of human nature can prosper. Instead of realising politicians wrestle with both the angel and the serpent in each of us, Titmuss' welfare cornerstone was made from altruism operating to a degree that is not always achieved in families.[28]

This sanitised post-Christian view of human character

held by Titmuss resulted in an approach to welfare which helped make Labour unelectable for so much of my political career. It has been the Titmuss legacy which I have opposed as being as dangerous as it is futile. Again I stress I do not see this as a minor issue. Nor do I feel I have blown it up out of all proportion. The Titmuss legacy lingered over the political debate with such force that I, for one, felt that it covered me with a form of intellectual treacle which made movement difficult. It precluded a proper discussion of fraud and this alone helped destroy Labour's credibility with street-wise voters who consequently did not consider Labour a party fit for the task of governing. Much worse, it immobilised Labour thinking as the political curtain began to sweep across the stage of state collectivism. Instead of leapfrogging the debate – such as with council house sales – and shaping the reform into one which increased housing opportunities generally, not just for richer tenants, Labour limped badly behind the political pack.[29] In place of repositioning the individual and the state by the development of new forms of collective activity which offered personal stakes and ownership, Labour allowed the electorate only the Thatcherite choice and then blamed them for taking it. In joining battle here I am not seeking to exaggerate differences with post-war orthodoxy. I see the Titmuss legacy as establishing a post-war orthodoxy which, while beneficial in the age of the ration book, became an intellectual, political and moral cul-de-sac into which Labour was manoeuvred during so much of the latter post-war period.

Conclusion

I have attempted to peer back through the looking-glass Deacon has held up to my work. The political strategy implicit in the three volumes I cited at the beginning are a combination of what Lord Plant sees as a top-down and bottom-up approach to political reform. What can be achieved by both approaches is, I believe, much more limited than the proponents of either school wish to believe. A top-down approach can set a framework which either works with or against the grain of human nature. The aim of the reforms I suggest is for a legislative framework which positively encourages the exercise of those verities centring around work, savings and honesty. Implicit here is my belief that the vast majority of us fall into the second category of Self as defined by Marquand, i.e. we see life as where our personal development is, viewed in terms of achieving more noble and civilised characters. Politicians can do very little in the short run to induce what appears to be naturally implanted instincts; they can do much, however, to prevent their flowering.

The ideas in *Making Welfare Work* and *How to Pay for the Future* are about a political programme in which welfare keeps to the current planned level of public provision, but seeks new ways for individuals to add to this. Current provision is defended because of its importance to the poor, although, all along, I have stressed that a welfare strategy can only succeed if it caters for the needs of the majority. Exclusion of the poor spells political disaster, and much of the debate from the 1960s onwards, with its exclusive concern for the poor, helped undermine popular support for the welfare state.[30] The poor's interest generally can only be advanced if the majority of voters see the relevance of the programme for them and their families.

The views I have espoused therefore do not fit easily into the category of those of the new age of moral collectivism which Marquand describes. There is redistribution, but not in the traditional way he defines. It is on this front that Deacon misreads the role I see for redistribution. My attack on the old formula of increasing taxes to spend on public services, where the individual's choice is merely to accept or reject what is offered, does not mean that redistribution is not part of my scheme of events. It has to be. But increasing redistribution is about personal ownership of the funds which result. This is not advanced simply because no other option is available – although I believe that to be true – but because the personal ownership fits in with the second ideal of Self as described by Marquand.

All these ideas are set within a belief about human nature. There is nothing original whatsoever about them if a time-span of a millennium is considered. What is new perhaps is the importance given to human nature from someone writing from the centre-left. This approach challenges the ascendancy which the role of altruism was seen to play in welfare. The difference is not marginal. Altruism was made the cornerstone of the post-war welfare state by the LSE ideologues. The travail into which this approach led the political debate is there for all those who choose to see it.

3: The Dependency Debate and New Directions in the United Kingdom

Speech given at the Beyond Dependency Conference:
A Watershed for Welfare,[31]
Auckland, New Zealand, March 16th–19th, 1997

The attack on the welfare dependency culture should be seen primarily as a strategy increasing the opportunities open to claimants. The main proposals I will make here include:

- Every able-bodied claimant would be expected to take part-time work as opportunities presented themselves. Each claimant would be given a bank or giro account into which they would pay part-time earnings, which would also keep details of their benefit payments. Part of these savings would be drawn down at the start of the school year, during school holidays and at Christmas. Most of the savings, however, would be kept and given to claimants as a capital sum when they start full-time work.
- Every single mother with children over four will be expected to look for work or undertake training. Once child care is available (paid for by privatising student grants and levying a graduate tax to repay this money) most single mothers on benefit would do what a minority of single mothers already do, i.e. work. Work would become the norm. Peer group pressure will then begin to operate. In addition, a much reduced case load for income support will allow staff to provide individual help and encouragement to single mothers making the transfer from benefit to training and work.
- Universalising Project Work will lead to major benefit savings. So far about 50 per cent of claimants refuse the offers made under project work and cease to claim benefit. Large parts of these savings should be used to finance jobs for the long-term unemployed.

- Welfare reform and education must go hand in hand. The supply routes to the underclass must be cut by raising educational performance in schools. In particular, under-achieving young female pupils need special attention as it is from this group that a disproportionately large number of unmarried single mothers come. Similarly, school leaving should be linked to achieving certain minimal educational and social skills. In today's labour market those young people leaving school without a good grasp of numeracy and literacy, and without IT and social skills, are likely to make up most of tomorrow's long-term chronic unemployed.

There are four further points I will also add. First, I wish to stress that this debate about welfare dependency rests on a simple, but I believe important truth, namely, that welfare provisions affect both people's behaviour and thereby their character. Second, in post-war Britain, that simple, but great truth about welfare's impact on character was not so much ignored, as denied. In its place an assumption was elevated that welfare provision allowed the altruism we try to practise within the family to operate on the great stage of public affairs. Third, welfare institutions are not morally neutral. They teach values. And finally, I would like to report where the dependency debate is in Britain and how I hope it will develop during the next parliament. I shall concentrate on this theme. In doing so I want to suggest why the temper of the dependency debate needs to be changed dramatically. Piecemeal reform may minimise political risk. But such an approach is unlikely to confront, let alone overthrow, a whole culture. Welfare reforms need to be dramatic in signalling the end of welfare dependency by the able-bodied adults of working age.

I will look first at the strange death of the welfare dependency debate in British politics and at its recent resurrection. During much of the last four hundred years the Poor Law in Britain tried to hold a balance between safeguarding public funds against unnecessary or self-induced welfare dependency, while at the same time giving equal emphasis to preserving the legitimate needs of the poor.

For most of our history, incomes from work did not permit personal savings. Dependency for the elderly was an accepted, honourable estate which the rest of society did not merely acknowledge, but also acted upon. For centuries a locally administered Poor Law ran what today would be called an unfunded pension scheme. In villages, all the elderly residents, barring the squire and the parson, were likely to be beneficiaries. Even in urban society, something like two-thirds of the population both drew and expected to draw a Poor Law pension.

Welfare provision for those of working age was similarly based on how people could and would respond to opportunities around them. The welfare offered would affect behaviour. Thus, the welfare system needed to be properly policed and send out clear messages of what was deemed responsible behaviour.

Post-war Britain lost sight of these most fundamental assumptions of running welfare. There are a number of reasons for this:

- The war era saw a pulling-together of the nation after the particularly divisive years of the inter-war period. The welfare reforms aimed to embody this new-found harmony.
- There was a strong Whig contingent in Whitehall which believed in the inevitability of progress – including the development of human nature – and these views were held despite the horrors made public as the concentration camps were overrun by Allied troops.
- The ethical basis underlying socialism lost a Christian perspective. Fallen man was replaced by one where human nature could be perfected. It became politically incorrect for the Left to question this stance. And the Tories – fearful of resurrecting their uncaring 1930s image that cost them so dearly in the 1945 election – lacked the courage to say that the new king had few garments.
- Each of these factors was reinforced by the philosophical framework promoted by the emerging social administration discipline. Generations of students – future leaders and foot soldiers in both the political and social field – were nurtured on a philosophic diet which emphasised the primacy of altruism in the right conduct of human affairs. This secularised version of the heavenly city quickly filled the space left by the retreat of Christian values.

So why was the whistle not blown earlier? The answer is disarmingly simple. Britain entered the golden years of full employment. Had anyone blown the whistle, people were too busy to listen. In addition it was seriously believed that we were about to enter a world where the problem would be the distribution of plenty, rather than the age-old issue of rationing scarce resources.

The position, as we approach the millennium, is different from this utopia in two most fundamental respects. Long-term unemployment is back with a vengeance. And more children are on welfare as a result of family break-up – or having no family in the first place – than as a result of having unemployed parents.

Major changes in the labour market, apparent by the early 1970s, called for a new approach. The nature of unemployment changed. When the post-war British economy was once again subjected to a process of boom and bust, the unemployed merely had to await the upturn. More often than not the unemployed went back to the same firm, and often to the same bench at which they had previously worked. Now, all too often, unemployment is caused by a firm's closure or its permanent reduction of its workforce. Re-employment, if and when it comes, will be with a totally new establishment.

The balance of the kind of work available has also changed. This trend should not be magnified out of all proportion. There is, however, a clear shift from a labour market where manual strength and dexterity are demanded, to one where numeracy and literacy, together with social and IT skills, are fundamental to a job. Both these changes – and others too – demand a proactive labour market policy.

A third of manufacturing industry has been wiped out in Britain since 1979. The loss of these jobs has left – like beached whales – large numbers of semi-skilled males with up to twenty or more years of their working life ahead of them. Similarly, the loss of these jobs has affected the chances of non-academic school leavers in finding work.

Initially the government targeted policy in the wrong direction. In order to save civil service posts, the age-old procedure of requiring claimants to register for work as a precondition of drawing benefit ceased. There are no prizes for prophesying the result.

From such crass beginnings the government began moving away from the objective of policy as cutting down the size of the civil service - whatever the consequences - to a proactive labour market stance. The first significant breakthrough on this front came in 1986 with the introduction of 'Restart'. Put simply this meant that claimants drawing benefit for six months would be required to attend an interview. Named appropriately Restart, the interview was aimed at helping claimants focus on the most effective ways of getting back into the labour market.

While a number of other initiatives have taken place since, the most important has been the beginnings of what Americans would call 'Workfare'. Pilot programmes – now called Project Work – have been initiated. The early returns show that, once offered a place on Project Work, around 50 per cent of the claimants subsequently ceased to draw benefit.

Only a very small minority are shown to have taken a job. But the returns do suggest that the extent of fraud – of people drawing benefit and working at the same time – is as extensive as some of the critics have maintained. Why has it been so difficult to establish this point? State-run welfare affected the attitude of taxpayers to fraud. All too many witnesses of fraud turned a blind eye. It was the state's problem and individual citizens felt they had no responsibility to help police the system. This shows how welfare institutions are not morally neutral; they can teach values which are corrosive to the good society.

As Project Work is extended to the whole country – it is currently being piloted in twenty localities – the benefit savings will be very substantial. At this point the welfare debate will divide along new lines. There will be those who will merely push for tax cuts financed by the welfare savings, believing jobs will come from a low taxed economy. Others will insist that a large proportion of the savings is used to begin to build up a range of jobs, valuable to local communities, which can be made available to those unable to gain much from training courses.

At this point the dependency debate will come full circle. When the modern debate on unemployment erupted into British politics in the late 1880s, Make Work schemes, as they were called, began to operate as a major source of relief. But these innovatory initiatives are rarely mentioned in the standard welfare texts, and when they are, they are invariably mocked and their worth minimised. It is left to conjecture just how good governments would be at Make Work schemes had this strategy been as intelligently developed over the century as it has been consistently denigrated. The new fault line in welfare politics will be between proponents and opponents who urge a practical rather than a benefit style responsibility to the most disadvantaged trying to enter or re-enter the labour market.

There is another reason why a new approach to dependency is urgently required. The composition of welfare rolls has changed – dramatically. Until very recently the dependency debate centred on the unemployed. Most of the effort at helping claimants return to work is still directed at this group. Yet benefits to single parents are more costly than those paid to the unemployed. More importantly, between four and five times more children grow up in single parent households on welfare than children in unemployed households.

Britain's single family population differs in important respects from its counterpart in European Union countries; it is not only relatively larger, but is also younger and has a higher proportion of never-married mothers. This age difference probably helps to explain why in Britain a smaller proportion of single parents work than in Europe. Most single mothers who start their families in their teens have never worked. They have no contact with the world of work. They have fewer qualifications than older single mothers and no firsthand experience of the network of contacts which help individuals find work.

This is not true for older single mothers, the overwhelming majority of whom are separated or divorced. This group has had a work history before they became mothers and for all the obvious reasons returning to work is easier for them than for those single mothers who have never worked.

Here I want to suggest a change in emphasis in the debate. Anti-dependency strategies all too often sound, at best, like policies of doing good to the poor and, at worst, introducing some stern discipline into the life of the indolent poor. Painting single mothers on welfare in a single colour gives a distorted monochrome image. A sizeable group of single mothers in Britain work, many going to extraordinary lengths to do so. They wish to establish noble role models for their children. A major aim of policy must be to salute these mothers and spread their success more widely.

A great barrier in the way of spreading this success is the lack of child care. We now live in an age of restive taxpayers. The politicians' normal response of putting their hands in the pockets of taxpayers and extracting yet more tax no longer holds. Instead politicians wishing to initiate new programmes must seek to reorder existing budgets. Privatising all student grants, so that the private sector finances these grants and the government claws back the cost from graduates by way of a graduate tax, would free around £1.2 billion of public funds. This sum should then be used to finance the universalisation of child care and nursery facilities.

This will result in a mass exodus of single parents from the welfare rolls. Others might be more diffident at accepting the challenge. Yet the greater the exodus the greater the peer group pressure will be for others to behave in a similar fashion. And the fewer mothers on the welfare rolls the more quickly a more proactive policy can be financed.

When single mothers first register for benefit, they should be invited to view their registration as the first day of the rest of their lives. Mothers with children over four years (when nursery education and child care facilities will be available) will be expected to work, and should be asked to begin thinking about what they want to achieve. Over time, the welfare staff would begin to build up the skills to help mothers achieve these objectives. A welfare budget which has ceased to grow out of control will also begin to be transformed into an investment and skills budget.

In this way the existing welfare culture begins to disintegrate and the number of single mothers on benefit falls. Peer group pressure begins to build new values centred around work, and these values are once again seen as the norm. All single mothers coming on to the welfare roll will be helped to think about what they want to achieve for the rest of their lives.

Welfare rules need a fundamental reordering in another respect. Too many of them operate against the grain of human nature. The great driving force for survival within each of us is now too often pitted against a regimentation of social security rules pushing in the opposite direction. If there was no welfare state, those of us becoming unemployed, for example, would scuttle around finding some work here, a few hours' work there. In this way, we would either attempt to build up a portfolio of work – to use the current jargon – or, more probably, hope eventually to find a full-time job – if that is what we wanted.

Today's welfare rules stop this natural process working. They operate to block the very process we should be aiming to achieve – maximising a person's natural instincts to leave the welfare roll. For this to happen to the best effect welfare has to operate as a bridge. All too often it now plays the role of a drawbridge trapping people into very long-term dependency.

Welfare rules need to change to make honesty easier, and to ensure that decent natural human instincts are allowed to flourish. All claimants working part-time – single parents and the unemployed – should be given a bank or giro account into which they would pay any earnings from part-time work over and above the level of disregarded earnings. The expectation would be that all able-bodied claimants would take part-time work as and when it was available. At the beginning the scheme could be offered on an experimental basis to those claimants who immediately wished to join in the reform. They would know a proportion of their savings could be drawn down at the beginning of the school year to help kit out their children, and also to meet the extra expenses at Christmas and holiday times. But the vast majority of the savings will be kept for the claimant as she or he leaves income support and works full-time.

Next, counter-dependency strategies must march hand in hand with education reforms. Education reforms must aim to cut the supply routes to very young single parenthood and the underclass of employed unskilled young males. Countering welfare dependency has to be broadened out from its traditional framework to one which embraces educational change.

In Britain the significant number of very young single mothers come predominantly from two groups of school girls: those who were high achievers up to the age of eleven, and then, when transferred to secondary school, begin to fail; and those who have always seen themselves as failures at school. The regular testing of pupils which now occurs in all

British schools must be refined in such a way that failure to perform well, or to cease performing well, sends out the appropriate red light signal, and that these red lights are read with particular care for female students who are failing to achieve. The transfer from primary to secondary schools has to be seen as the danger zone it is for all too many pupils.

Similarly, the supply routes to young unskilled unemployable males need to be cut. In Britain there are currently 1.2 million individuals who have never worked since leaving school. To leave school with neither basic numeracy and literacy nor IT and social skills, is an almost certain recipe for unemployment. Instead of having an arbitrary school leaving age, eligibility for leaving school should be defined by way of acquiring these basic minimum skills.

Let me conclude by emphasing three aspects of this debate. First, welfare must be seen as having an impact on the motivation and behaviour of claimants. Being the costliest part of the government budget, welfare has enormous potential for good or ill. The question is no longer 'does welfare affect values?' but what action should it promote and nurture. When put like this, most people would suggest work, savings and honesty, and that the greatest of these three is work. Just as it is in the shadow of the bay tree that we grow good, so, from the protection offered by work, savings and honesty can prosper.

Second, conventional welfare wisdom awaits to be overthrown. Paying benefits is not where the duties of civil society cease. Welfare must be reshaped from a passive to a proactive agency.

Third, the supply routes to dependency must be cut. For this to become a meaningful strategy it is necessary to see education reforms playing an increasingly important part. The supply routes to very young single motherhood must be blocked. So, too, must we ensure that schools cease to produce large numbers of unskilled males for whom chronic long-term unemployment is the only legitimate goal to which they can look forward.

4: Welfare:
New Labour Markets
and Fiscal Reform

Institute of Directors Annual Lecture,
delivered February 27th 1997, London, SW1

How can Labour be serious about tackling poverty if it is not prepared to spend more money? That is the charge which is already being made. By failing to make such a commitment Labour is further charged with adopting Tory welfare reforms.

The irony here is that if spending more money on welfare is seen as the litmus test of concern for the poor, radicalism and Christian commitment, then clearly the Tories are the party to vote for. Under the Tory government, money is currently being spent on welfare as though there is no tomorrow. Welfare is not only the largest but has, under Mrs Thatcher and John Major, been the fastest growing part of the government's budget.

Labour's approach is radically different from the old-style welfare debate and equally different from the Conservative Party's approach. Tony Blair has accepted that one test of a Blair government will be how the position of the poor is improved. But success is not to be measured in the growth in the welfare budget, but in how new and worthwhile opportunities are created for the poor.

A hand-up, not a put-down welfare is the goal. This will involve a revolutionary approach to those of working age who are on benefit. The aim is:

- to abolish finally the Poor Law which has always required that the able-bodied be excluded from the labour market if they are to receive help
- to turn what is essentially a passive welfare state into a proactive operation of national renewal
- to strike a new balance between community and

individual responsibility
- to ensure that self-improvement once again becomes a great engine-force for social and economic advance
- to direct self-interest so that it simultaneously promotes general well-being.

Labour's new welfare is also based on two things: changes in the economy – although these changes are different, I believe, from the analysis which is regularly relayed through the media; and changes in our political culture which are having an impact on the operation and scope of government and thereby welfare.

Let me begin with the changes in the economy which are impacting on welfare. It is almost impossible to pick up a newspaper or listen to the media and not be told that we are being buffeted by a jobs revolution. We are constantly being told how the age-old employment patterns have changed forever. This maelstrom is of such force and ferocity that almost no job is now safe. A job for life is now no more than a flickering memory – like buttered Hovis at nursery tea-time.

Were most jobs ever that secure even in the age of full employment? Throughout the first forty years of this century the bottom end of the labour market was excluded from the discussion. It was brushed aside. It was merely the residuum and not worthy of consideration. The lot of this large group of unskilled workers was unemployment punctuated by spells of casual labour.

Was there even stability – jobs for life – among mainstream workers? Hardly. The 1911 Insurance Act was itself a response to an economy which swung quickly from boom to recession and back again to boom. Hence the importance of insurance against short spells of unemployment. Even if we limit ourselves to the work records of today's pensioners the picture is one of job changes in order to earn the daily bread. Today's male pensioners have had an average between 7.1 and 8 jobs through their working lives – depending on income – and up to an average of 1.3 spells of unemployment. Today's women pensioners have held on average between 5 and 5.9 jobs and experienced around two spells of unemployment. If the average is between seven and eight jobs for men, what must be the range? From one job – that elusive ideal – to perhaps fifteen to twenty, or twenty-five jobs during the working life, I would guess. These figures are from the record of many, although not all, pensioners who benefited from the golden years of post-war full employment.

If we bring into focus a snapshot of jobs – rather than a moving picture of those who held jobs – we find some change, but it is rather modest compared with the picture which is normally developed. In 1975 the shelf life for male jobs averaged nineteen years. By 1992 it had fallen to seventeen years. For women workers the shelf-life of jobs remains around twelve years.

Averages can of course be misleading. But there is still a stability and certainty in the labour market which is not even hinted at in the current debate. That does not mean, of course, that some workers are not unemployed – too many are. There are others who feel insecure, many obviously do, or others who have to take unsatisfactory jobs – but it was sadly ever thus.

But, some will exclaim, the rise and rise of part-time work constitutes a flexibility and, by inference, a casualisation I appear to be denying. But isn't much of this a flexibility which both employer and worker wish? Let us examine this proposition step by step. The growth in part-time work has certainly been dramatic – up from 4 per cent of the workforce in 1951 to 22 per cent forty years later. The definition of part-time work has also changed as far as employers go. It used to be thirty-two or thirty hours a week. Now part-time jobs can be any number of hours – some quite few. And a price has been paid for this flexibility: the drastic cutting of the income of part-time workers. Even so, nine out of ten people who work part-time want to do so – the same as the average in OECD countries – even if the take-home pay is less than the level part-time work used to pay. These part-time workers need a flexibility to manage their other responsibilities which overwhelmingly centre on giving care for children or an elderly relative. Employers often need the flexibility to meet the uneven flows of demand for their product. The growth in part-time work during the 1990s is roughly the same as in the 1980s. The big increase came during the 1970s when there was a significant increase in the numbers of working women.

Even an analysis of the length of time part-time jobs are held does not immediately offer itself to the doom and gloom scenario of the British labour market. Two thirds of part-timers have been with the same employer for two years and two in five have had the same employer for more than five years. Even the number of temporary jobs shows little change over the past decade.

So a sense of balance needs to be introduced. There are clearly far too many workers who have been marginalised, far too many who have seen living standards rise less fast than in the past and far too many who have been unemployed. But these regrettable circumstances do not give the total picture of British labour market changes. The great British pleasure of irrationally feeling we are about to be overwhelmed by dark and mighty forces must be resisted. The debate needs to be refocused onto the five major changes in the labour market's operation which are having a severe impact on people's lives and therefore indirectly on the welfare they require.

The collapse of manufacturing industry

As societies get richer the size of their manufacturing employment falls. But crass exchange rate policies, combined with a manic reliance on inappropriate fiscal and monetary stances, speeded up this process in the 1980s above what would otherwise have been the rate of change. One third of manufacturing jobs have been wiped out since 1979. Overwhelmingly, these were male jobs, and generally they were jobs paying at least a semblance of a family wage. Society cannot expect a mass of happy families in which to nurture children if the wage system is moving away from producing family wages.

Increase in self-employment

Second, there has been an increase in self-employment to

such a degree that I believe it has begun to make a seismic change in work patterns. In the eleven years from 1979, self-employment almost doubled; up from 7.5 per cent to 13 per cent of the total work-force. It is this sector which is most vulnerable to swings in economic activity, and those swings, and with them bankruptcies, have done much to engender a feeling of widespread insecurity. This failure of a proper management of the economy has also bruised much potential entrepreneurial spirit. How many of today's young people, seeing what happened to their parents who responded eagerly to Mrs Thatcher's clarion call for an entrepreneurial renaissance, now consider it wise to follow where their parents' footsteps led? An economy with a large self-employed sector needs a much more sensitive and intelligent exchange rate, monetary and fiscal policy than we have yet seen, even under the moderately sensible hand of Kenneth Clarke. It also requires a different welfare system from one where the vast majority are employees.

Unfair spread of work

Jobs are now much more unfairly spread between households and the pay of jobs which allow entry or re-entry into the labour market has fallen – usually relatively and sometimes absolutely.

Change on this front has also been dramatic. In 1979 most new jobs went to members of a household where no-one else was in work. Today these new job vacancies go overwhelmingly to individuals who come from households where at least one other person is in work.

There are two major causes of this unequal spread of new

jobs. The pay of these jobs is such that they are unattractive to breadwinners where everyone else at home is without work. Conversely the pay is not that low to put off applicants from homes where other pay cheques regularly arrive.

The social security rules play a destructive and negative role in reinforcing the great jobs divide. As soon as a breadwinner exhausts the right to insurance benefits, the means-tested help available destroys any financial incentive for wives or partners to continue working. Indeed many families become substantially better off if the wife opts out of employment and joins her husband in the dole queue.

Decline in activity rates for older workers

Fourth, there has been a decline in what are called the activity rates of male workers. In contrast those for women workers have continued to increase, even for women approaching retirement.

The loss of the manufacturing jobs I mentioned earlier helps to explain the rise in inactivity rates among males aged fifty-five years and above. The loss of these jobs also helps us explain the rise in the nomadic young unskilled males with no jobs to go to, who move quickly between partners, and who often combine social security fraud and crime in order to establish some identity role and a higher income.

But surpluses in pension funds provided a big sweetener to what is now euphemistically called 'downsizing', and which used to be called sackings. While life for the 640,000 males below state pensionable age drawing occupational pensions may be fine, the danger is that such early retirements have helped to reinforce a view that such a pattern of retirement is and should be the norm. Logically it cannot be if we are to continue to live longer, to have more and more active years in retirement, and then, sometimes, to need intensive care at the end of our very long lives. There simply is not enough wealth for that scenario to have a happy ending for most early retired. For a given level of pension, a person retiring at sixty, instead of sixty-five, requires twice the capital to be able to draw the same sized pension.

The rise of the long-term unemployed

Fifth, there are again among us the long-term unemployed. Just how serious the issue is I cannot say. We no longer have records. We used to, but when income support replaced supplementary benefits in 1988 no link was made in the records. So we have a government which endlessly rails on about welfare dependency – rightly I think – but has been so wilfully careless about the need to report accurately to taxpayers on their stewardship, that we cannot say how many individuals and families have been on welfare for fifteen, twenty, twenty-five or thirty years. Like the deadly charge Dr Zhivago levelled against the Bolsheviks after the death of Lara, it was the arch proponents of central planning who were so careless, and so inefficient, that they did not know where the evil deed was done.

But the very long-term unemployed exist, even if no official record is kept or if they have been reclassified as long-term sick and disabled. Nor can we be confident that this group will diminish thanks to an economy which continues to produce more jobs, or recruits into retirement as the grim reaper beckons. There is a clear supply route to perpetual unemployment. Here records do exist. There are 1.2 million individuals who have never worked since leaving school, and this total excludes those who are currently students and who will hopefully soon pass into the labour market.

Before looking at the agenda for reform I want to touch on those changes in our political culture which, along with changes in the economy, set a framework within which any welfare reforms have to be recast. Here there are three important forces at work.

1. Hardening of hearts

I can best describe the first force as nothing less than a hardening of the public's heart. But hardening against what? There is quite a cocktail involved. The repositioning of self-interest to its proper central place in affairs was conducted with such enthusiasm that the less subtle minds among us could have mistaken it as a drive to selfishness, if not towards greed. Proper self-interest has become so hedged around by forms of self-centredness that this natural impulse itself is being distorted. There is also an understandable disappointment that, while the welfare bill is high and continues to grow out of control, there is no apparent social advance to justify this vast expenditure. Worse still, many see much of welfare as part of the problem, and not as its solution. Ignoring people's concern on this front as the Left used to do or, worse still, denying that many voters see this as an issue, helps to turn a genuine question into a spiralling cynicism against politicians, the political process and most forms of public good.

The reserves of the public sense of decency and propriety need to be rebuilt. I can only hint at how this might be achieved. How politicians behave, how they talk with, rather than hector at voters, how often they admit mistakes instead of hiding behind vacuous barricades, all have a part to play. How good they are at their duties in managing public finances is also important. The effective spending of existing budgets is also crucial in helping to re-establish trust with the electorate. Before the electorate backs any sweeping reforms, which may need extra funding in the short run in order to win long-term savings, public confidence to such an approach has to be earned.

2. Resistance to tax increases

As I have called for more honesty in admitting mistakes let me do just that. For too long I accepted the Crosland idea that as incomes rose the resistance to tax levels would fall. This may sound a simple if fundamental error but its acceptance contains a revolution in centre left thinking. Let me unpack such a broad assertion.

As a country's national income increases, the amount spent on food falls – in short, Engel's Law. This occurs during the first stage of economic development. Then there is a second stage where public services, however delivered, usually paid for by somebody else, offer substantial gains in living standards for recipients.

The third stage – one in which we are now – comes when continual increases in income begin to offer people real choices to spend more on health, education and pensions, as well as holidays, entertainment, housing or simply eating out. Nor is it on the additional income on which individuals want much more say. How services are delivered becomes part of the end itself. But that is not all. Because income rises now take an ever-growing proportion of the population into the world of real choices, there is a growing resistance to current tax levels, never mind an increase in them. Our politics have yet to experience the full impact of what might be called the financial coming of age of the British taxpayer.

3. Fraying inter-generational trust

The third force is inter-generational trust. This is most clearly seen by my payment of taxes for another's benefits in the belief that future generations of taxpayers will in turn pay my benefits. This trust is not a free good. The reliability of the unwritten part of this pact is being flushed out in public debate. Will future taxpayers – many of them not yet born – be as willing a group of taxpayers as we are? A question mark has been registered.

What policies should be drawn from this analysis? First, the trust which exists between generations, and which much of our social security system takes for granted, must be valued as a scarce resource. It should not be dissipated on further state pension initiatives, when increasingly people are making their own second funded provision. Second, resistance to direct tax increases are a fact of life, not a momentary aberration. The age of the passive taxpayer is, in the words describing the death of George v, moving peacefully towards its close. Whether they like it or not, governments will have to negotiate tax changes move by move with the electorate. Third, there will be a continual movement away from central state provision to a mixture of private and collective provision – this latter provision having nothing whatsoever to do with state provision. Moreover a new partnership between the individual and the collective will be struck, but the collective will be advancing new forms of non-state provision, and the individual ownership itself will begin to reshape the governance of the private sector. I will now suggest how I think welfare will respond within this framework to the major changes in the economy which I highlighted earlier.

First pensions. The Institute of Directors has recently added its weight to the growing consensus of compulsory universal second-funded provision. If this move is to be successful a simplification of pensions regulations will be required. Paying contributions into a pension scheme should be as simple and as easy to understand as depositing money in a building society. You do not see many advertisements telling customers how to deposit their savings in this sector – or to understand the current value of their deposited assets.

What form should the simplification take? It must encompass:

• a new single tax regime

- a simple tax allowance account equal for every contributor, which rolls over from year to year, and which will revolutionise the Revenue's role
- the Revenue's policing activities on past payments, which largely catch people who make genuine mistakes, should cease. It should concentrate instead on serious fraud.

The reform must also allow:

- husbands and wives, and partners too, to make payments into each other's pension accounts
- capital windfalls from gambling and inheritance to be paid into the accounts with normal tax advantages
- greater flexibility for the young. Let us make savings for a pension one of the most natural things in the world. Should it not be possible to open pension accounts for children, so that grandparents, godparents, half-brothers and half-sisters, and uncle Tom Cobbley if he so wishes, can make contributions?

These new pension savings accounts will be run by mutually aided associations and private companies. The key factor will be individuals insistence on the personal ownership of their savings.

While these reforms will obviously help those with varying and fluctuating incomes – particularly the self-employed and part-timers – they will also be of value to the majority and will thereby win widespread support.

The second set of reforms must aim to cut the supply routes to Britain's growing underclass – very young single mothers and the long-term unemployed. Here the forging of a totally new contract between education and welfare reform becomes most obvious.

Britain has a higher proportion of single mothers than most other countries and in Britain single mothers are generally younger. While we cannot predict who will become a very young unmarried mother we know the two groups from which the overwhelming majority of such mothers are drawn. They are: girls who were achieving up to the age of eleven and who then cease to be achievers; and girls who have always seen themselves as underachievers. The growth of regular school tests must be used to raise the achievements of all pupils, but in particular of these two groups.

The whole benefit culture also needs to be changed. Governments have allowed a system to build up which can best be described as a resting place, rather than a springboard back into the labour market. This is particularly so with single mothers – many of whom feel and are trapped on benefit.

Under current rules a single mother is not required to register for work until her youngest child is sixteen. This must change. If student grants were privatised, and the private sector repaid through the collection of a graduate tax, £1.2 billion would be made available for nursery and childcare facilities.

Such a switchover of existing resources within the education budget would allow income support to be revolutionised. Each single mother registering for benefit would be told that this was the first day of the rest of her life.

How would she like to spend her time on income support; acquiring the skills or work opportunities, so as to become self-sufficient again? The vast majority of single mothers would jump at such an opportunity. By responding positively, the existing welfare culture will begin to disintegrate. Peer group culture would then come into play against those single mothers who have succumbed to welfare dependency.

The supply route to the nomadic young unskilled unemployed male must similarly be cut. Unskilled, largely illiterate, young males leaving school are now almost guaranteed a life of unemployment. There is little point moving into the labour market without basic numeracy, literacy, IT and social skills. The aim must be for every normal child to achieve a basic set of skills which make a life at work a possibility. One way of signifying the change here, and why it is imperative to achieve at the very least a set minimum standard, is for the school leaving age to be attached to gaining these qualifications, rather than be arbitrarily linked to a specific age.

While I am aware that these changes are being presented in a headline form I am not without appreciation of the range of other reforms which are necessary to make their achievement possible. Welfare must also be reformed so as to spread the new jobs between more households, rather than concentrate jobs in households where members are already working, which is what is happening at present. As I have already commented, once a breadwinner is out of work, it usually pays for their partner not to work. Part, but only part, of the reason for this is that the starting pay of most jobs is low and the jobs' shelf-life is usually uncertain. It does not pay to take the risk.

We must begin to reward taking a risk through the benefit system. If unemployment insurance was recast so that eligibility to benefit was regained after twelve weeks back at work – instead of the current two year qualification period – the social security system would be giving both a powerful incentive, as well as signalling publicly what sort of behaviour is valued and therefore rewarded.

Let me suggest one last reform and one which employers can do more to shape than other groups. The reason I have discussed at length what I believed was actually happening in the economy, and not what was so commonly presented in the media, is that the current debate based on fallacious assumptions is influencing policy and doing so in a distorted and negative manner.

One industry where a job for life has very often been replaced by a limited contract is, ironically, the media. Not unnaturally this group of workers has been prone to see their treatment as similarly operating elsewhere, and is anxious to report the scope of such changes. The idea of the spread of a flexible, casual, labour force, working part-time and too often on insecure contracts, is hence increasingly seen as the norm and, more importantly, is shaping policy. Here a vicious circle is being created. A brave new world is arising from the belief that downsizing is the norm, full-time permanent jobs are a thing of the past, contract work is the norm and retirement in the early fifties is standard in the new life. Then the beliefs become a self-fulfilling prophesy.

This near-universal adoption of 'copycat' employment

strategies needs to be challenged. It would be valuable if this organisation led the debate and thereby introduced a much needed sense of balance. There are several points to remember. Much of Britain's work-force has always been part of a flexible work-force in terms of moving between jobs, working non-standard hours and so on. There have been particular changes over the past two decades, and the debate on how society should respond must not be swamped by wild talk of a near total revolution by labour market Jeremiahs. The rapidly increasing self-employed sector should place a growing emphasis on the value of fine tuning the economy. Finally, the most valuable of most firms' capital is now in the heads of their employees, which makes the switch from welfare to education not only right in terms of the new opportunities it will begin to offer to the dispossessed, but makes sense for a country which knows how differently investment should be measured in the millennium.

5: Rebuilding Mutual Aid

Speech given to the UK Co-operative Council, Fifth Annual Forum,
Manchester, November 22nd 1996

Richard Titmuss set the scene. His view was that 'when we study welfare systems we see that they reflect the dominant cultural and political characteristics in their societies'.[32] Let us suppose for the moment that we see our welfare system through eyes trained by 'the dominant cultural and political characteristics' of our society.

In Britain, the dominant cultural and political characteristics all point in the same direction. In welfare, collectivism has been the order of the day. Moreover, this trend has been presented as inevitable. One writer characterised British history 'as if society was on a great collective train journey into the future'.

Now let us further suppose that such a crude Whig interpretation of history – seeing events developing in an inexorable linear progression – is profoundly mistaken. What if the process of history is better described as a tide, moving first one way and then the other, with intermittent periods of calm and others of great activity? Such a view would, for example, create a near revolutionary change in the way welfare's history is presented. The great collective train journey would still feature, but only as one part of a much wider picture. Most text books on welfare would need to be radically revised. Practically all of their titles tell of the coming of the welfare state. Thus the Whig concept of a story which has a beginning and a definite end reigns supreme.

Moreover, many of those who write on welfare issues give only a cursory glance, if any at all, to events before 1945. Such bias is of course understandable if history's story is a progression towards state welfare and that it stops there. But suppose the train's ultimate destination is not in reality the welfare state established by Mr Attlee and his colleagues. Let us assume that the welfare provision of the early post-war period, while it may have been the most suitable for that time, was no more than a response to a very specific period in our history, and was in no way a final resting place.

To question the traditional view that an optimal welfare state was predestined, and that it arrived with the coming of the near monopoly state provision in the early post-war period, affects today's debate in two important respects. First, it leads to a very different interpretation of recent welfare developments. Far from seeing every change in the post-war settlement as a retreat from or even a defeat of the idealised welfare system, reforms might be more properly viewed as attempts by consumers to create a more satisfactory welfare provision. Any change, of course, can hold out dangers for the weakest who can all too easily get left behind or even ignored. But it is difficult to argue that most changes by Conservative governments since 1979 have lacked electoral appeal.

Second, it underlines the weakness of how our welfare history is taught. Either events before 1945 are so unimportant they barely get a mention, or they are only of importance in describing how the train reached its destination with Mr Attlee on the footplate.

But if there is no abiding city for welfare – or anything else – and if our role as reformers and consumers can be compared to that of a pilgrim, ever willing to move and rarely constant, then past welfare history assumes a totally new importance. The task is then to know more about what went on before 1945, what worked and why, and what parts of these best past provisions can be refashioned and built upon to provide a more effective welfare system for the millennium.

Three lessons from our history become important in such an exercise of historical recovery. The first is that there was life, so to speak, before monopoly state provision, and that life will continue to exist and indeed develop as the role of the state changes. Much of that life before monopoly state provision was concerned with providing welfare on a collective, not on a state, basis. I cannot stress too strongly the importance of this distinction. Largely because of the widespread ignorance of welfare history before 1945, all too many of today's political activists present a polarisation between the state and private provision as the only means of delivering welfare. Historically this is simply not true.

The second lesson is that the form of collective provision based on mutual aid principles was one which believed welfare provision can never be a neutral activity as far as human motivation goes. Welfare affects behaviour for good or ill. Again this simple point needs stressing for it comes as a shock to all too many political activists – although not, I am glad to say, to voters and taxpayers. The centre left can unite in the campaign to limit tobacco advertising, for this we believe has too widespread and too deadly an effect on the behaviour of too many of us. But, ironically, the sharpest of arguments breaks out over whether a £95 billion welfare bill affects anyone's, let alone practically everyone's, behaviour.

The third and equally important lesson is that welfare imparts values, and here again is a great truth we need to draw from the pioneers of modern welfare. The co-operative and mutual aid movement did not merely preach values but lived them out in their everyday activity.

Fraternity has long been a seminal value in Labour's thinking. Liberty and equality mattered as objectives. But fraternity was the stuff of everyday life. It could make the difference between survival or simply going under. Trade unionism would have been stillborn had fraternity not acted as midwife. Strength to oppose the naked aggression of a new capitalism came from the sinking of individual ambitions into a nurturing of common objectives. Yet the fraternity of the branch did not end with trade union politics or with friendly society business. For necessity's sake, arguably, it became the weave and the web of most of everyday existence. The pooling of risks was as much the very stuff of the Friendly Society Movement, as it was in offering help to a neighbour facing an unexpected crisis.

There was nothing clinical then about the advent of modern fraternity. One of the finest of human motives – brotherhood – was hewn out of the crude politics of necessity. And yet the outcome – of a brotherhood underpinned by self-interest – was ennobling of the human character. Here was, in a very practical sense, loving one's neighbour as oneself. The second of the two great commandments. So not only are past means of delivering welfare relevant to today's debate on welfare reform. The values taught by these welfare systems are of equal importance to how Labour should reconstruct welfare for the millennium.

There is no going back to the world before Mrs Thatcher

left such an indelible mark upon it. Some of her changes, were for the good and are widely supported by the electorate. But in one respect at least, a perceived downside of Thatcherism needs to be confronted. Bluntly, Mrs Thatcher was right to reposition self-interest.

Self-interest is a paramount human drive. But if it is unbuttressed by other values it takes on a cancerous force. Unguarded, it can all too quickly disintegrate into selfishness, and selfishness is only a few steps away from greed. The outcome can be truly calamitous when the government encourages the electorate to break down the barriers between self-interest and selfishness and then again actively destroys the distinction between selfishness and greed.

It is easy enough to let the genie out of the bottle. It is quite another matter trying to tame it once it is unbridled. Self-interest does need to be tempered and this can only occur if it is buttressed by values which allow it to flourish in the manner which is advantageous to both the individual and the public.

Let me clarify this further. It is possible, indeed desirable, to encourage self-interest within a broader social context and to foster a realisation of responsibility towards a broader community. Here the reconstruction of welfare – which is taking place anyway – comes to our aid. Welfare is the largest of all government budgets – it towers over all other combined departmental budgets bar three. Welfare is clearly a powerful force for good or evil. Moreover, welfare's institutions can foster either indifference – as state-run bodies usually do – or to an even greater extent the 'I'm all right' philosophy. Alternatively it can build up a sense of common endeavour – and thereby the practice of fraternity – while simultaneously meeting two other crucial welfare objectives. These are increasing expenditure on welfare from current income (although some of this welfare expenditure will mean savings to spend later) and putting into place a more easily policed welfare system.

How can self-interest be repositioned in a reconstructed welfare system so that it simultaneously promotes the common good? Here values and institutional reform become inextricably linked. As I have already said, it is not a question of keeping the status quo. Reform is well under way. The question is whether we are going to let future reforms be Treasury-led – they have been for the last twenty years or so – or whether Labour is consciously going to reform welfare by criteria other than an exclusive concern with controlling expenditure levels – important as this is.

One of the great questions facing all governments, but particularly a Labour one, is how can adequate levels of common services be provided when taxpayers are understandably restive over current levels of tax? A new approach has to be found so that individuals allot more of their current income to welfare. I do not believe this can be achieved without offering those same individuals control over the schemes into which more of their money is allocated and, in respect of pensions, invested.

This means an alternative to the current drift of rugged self-centred individualism must be found which will offer the punters a new welfare contract based on a self-interest which will also promote the public good. Here organisations based on mutual aid come into their own. Such bodies are commercially run but differ from private companies in that there are no shareholders. The organisations are owned by their membership. There are profits – an index of success – but the profits go back into the firm in the form of better services to members, or in higher benefits, or both. The organisation therefore, and this is equally important, fosters a sense of fraternity which urgently needs to be strengthened in our society.

Mutual aid organisations are based on a fraternity which is fed by and in its turn feeds self-improvement. An advance in mutual aid will ensure that self-improvement once again becomes the great engine force for social advance. Welfare reconstruction cannot be based on a single principle alone. But one of the criteria by which a Labour government should judge reform is whether any proposal furthers the principle of mutual aid. This will be a deliberate choice, just as the Conservative Party has always made a choice to construct a playing field on which the private company is placed at no disadvantage.

The private sector will be a welcome and necessary partner in welfare reconstruction. But the rules of engagement will be set with the fostering of mutual aid organisations as paramount. The private sector will be welcome to compete on these new terms.

Substantial progress is already being made for reforms along these lines. Whether we like it or not, or indeed realise it or not, we are at the advent of a stakeholder society. Increasingly, individuals are demanding, and gaining, greater control over their own immediate lives in a world in which, at the same time, other decisions have to be made at a global or near global level.

One of the major reasons the franchise was extended to a universal basis in this country was that Victorians became convinced of the working man's worth – and somewhat later the working woman's – by the way the skilled and semi-skilled workers had gone about organising their own welfare states. One of the distinguishing characteristics of the nineteenth century was not so much self-help but mutual help. Indeed the great apostle of self-help, Samuel Smiles, blurs the distinction between these two activities in *Self-help* [33] – a book whose title carried his message into a multiplicity of countries.

But just as the success of the mutual aid movement helped persuade the Establishment to concede the vote on an ever-increasing scale because the so-called lower orders had shown they were worthy of it, so, too, at the same time did the spread and robustness of mutual aid organisations build crucial countervailing forces between the individual and the state. Now we live in an age when self-interest and self-help both need to be encouraged and directed in an incorporating manner, so that the least advantaged are not excluded. In an age of globalisation we are urgently required to rebuild institutions which give individuals an increasing sense of self-worth. Equally important, we need groups of association which give us a sense of time, locality and importance. This is particularly relevant when so many economic decisions are being taken by groups of individuals who feel no primary responsibility to time or national boundaries. Welcome again to the age of mutuality.

6: State-run War of Attrition on Self-improvement

The Allen Lane Foundation Memorial Lecture 1996,[34] delivered at Thomas Coram Foundation, London wc1, March 26th 1996.

Introduction

The social security budget is not only by far and away the largest of all central government programmes and the one which is growing fastest, but it is also one in which means-tested expenditure increasingly dominates. Means-tested benefit expenditure constitutes a threat not just to the probity of public finances but to the well ordering of civil society as well.

Means-tests have a destructive impact on individuals and the wider society. They have a corrupting influence on individuals. Means-tests penalise effort and initiative. They tax savings. They place a premium on honesty. Their overall impact on human character is a dangerous one. The great drive by the Tories to push people on to means-tested assistance is the biggest British state-run war of attrition on self-improvement in history.

Far from an undisguised blessing, the expanding welfare expenditure now constitutes a grave threat. The budget is not sustainable in the longer run. A major disengagement from state welfare will take place. The easiest and most popular way of achieving this outcome would be for a further disengagement from universal benefits, allowing the middle class to order their own welfare provision and a regimentation of the poor into ever more ghetto-type schemes.

How might this scenario be avoided? In my opinion mutual aid could play a significant role in:

• meeting the legitimate needs of the most affluent 80 per

cent for greater ownership and control, while at the same time preventing social security from entrenching an underclass at the lower levels of British society

- marrying together Labour's adherence to market principles with its historic commitment to common endeavours
- illustrating how the dominant power of self-interest can be channelled into a great engine force for self-improvement which has been shown to be the only successful way of securing long-term human advance
- seeing today's global market as no greater a threat than unbridled laissez-faire capitalism, itself successfully reformed by the mutual aid movement. Individuals freely combining together showed that they were a match for those economic developments. So too today.

Let us, at this point, indulge in a flight of fancy – imagine we have been transported back in time to 1979. Then consider your response to a lecturer who prophesied in 1979 that by 1996 the social security budget would have the following characteristics:

- the budget would total £90 billion and take a third of all taxpayers' revenue
- the social security bill which amounted in 1979 to 23 per cent of the total government budget would, by 1996, have cornered 31 per cent of a much enlarged budget
- the 9 per cent of GDP spent on social security in 1979 would, by 1996, have risen to 12.6 per cent
- that in the seventeen years following the 1978-79

financial year, social security expenditure would be set to grow by 470 per cent compared with an increase of 340 per cent in money GDP.

Now imagine the lecturer asks which party – Labour or Conservative – has been in power since this extraordinary rise in social security expenditure has occurred. Without doubt, I think most of us would have concluded only a Labour government could have produced social security growth figures like those I have just listed. These facts, in the real world of today, help to explain why the Conservatives are in a near-perpetual panic on the question of public expenditure.

The status quo therefore cannot hold. A number of mighty forces are beginning to draw up and aim their firepower against the social security budget. Change will be forced from a number of directions.

1: Size of growth
There is first the impact of the social security budget's sheer size and its extraordinary growth. No matter how it is measured, the social security budget is growing at a phenomenal rate. The Conservative Party has given up its aspiration to cut the budget in real terms. It now embraces only the modest goal of limiting social security expenditure's advance to below the underlying growth rate in the economy. The claims by the Secretary of State to have reduced the annual growth and to have set it on a path below the underlying growth rate in the economy, must be held against his own record, never mind that of the whole

government since 1979.

During the period of Peter Lilley's stewardship, the social security budget has each year burst through the limit agreed by the cabinet in its annual public expenditure round by at least £1 billion and often by £3 billion. To give an example – in the 1992 Autumn Statement the social security budget was increased by £1.3 billion. The Statement allowed for a further increase of over £900 million in 1993-94. In the 1993 budget, however, that total was increased by a further £2.3 billion. In other words the 1992 projection was increased by a further £3.2 billion. In 1994-95 the Autumn Statement projection of 1992 allowed for a further £600 million increase in social security. The 1993 budget added a further £1.6 billion to this total but a year later the 1994 budget had to add an additional £1.46 billion, i.e. an increase of over £3.6 billion.

Peter Lilley's latest estimate is for a growth rate of a little over 1 per cent. If social security continues to grow at the same rate it has done since Peter Lilley took charge, rather than what is now merely estimated, the social security budget will continue to grow faster than the growth in national income.

2: Attacking good government

A second attack on the social security budget has also opened on a different front. Its inexorable growth is preventing good government. Over the period 1992-93 to 1996-97, to take the period since Peter Lilley became Secretary of State only, public expenditure has grown by £43 billion, from the level of £263 billion up to a total of

£306 billion. Of this increase the social security programme, which already claims the largest share of the total budget, cornered the lion's share of the increase, or two-fifths of the total rise in government spending over the period. The sheer size and the apparent uncontrollability of the largest of public budgets makes it increasingly difficult for the government to prioritise expenditure over the range of its total programme. Aneurin Bevan once claimed that priorities were the language of socialism. They are certainly the basis of good government. Over the past seventeen years in particular, cabinet ministers to all intents and purposes have been taken prisoner by the imperial guard at the DSS, whose budget growth increasingly limits the ability of other ministers to take independent action.

3: More for less

The third force challenging the rise of social security expenditure stems from nothing less than a double paradox. Over wide tracts of public expenditure the government has introduced market-orientated reforms. Their aim was not only to gain better value for money, but also for those gains to cover the cost of any likely increase in demand for services. According to Nicholas Bosanquet's argument the impact of the reforms has been such, and the performance of the public sector so enhanced, that the reforms themselves have unleashed new swathes of demand.[35] The reforms have therefore had the opposite effect to the government's intention. This is the first paradox. The second is how any increase in the supply of public goods can be paid for. Whether or not it is a true reflection, practically all senior politicians believe that to suggest rises in direct taxation would court electoral disaster. Apart from printing money or borrowing, moves which would be immediately punished by the international capital market, the only alternative is indirect taxation. This is the paradox. Demands for an increase in public expenditure are most easily voiced by middle class groups, those with the sharp elbows, anxious to get themselves and their families to the top of the queue. The most expedient political way of paying for those increases is by indirect taxation which bears most heavily on poorer people. Increases in public expenditure paid for by poorer groups but disproportionately benefiting richer groups is a strategy a future radical government can hardly contemplate with ease.

4: Attack on character

The fourth attack which is well and truly opening up against the status quo is the impact of means-tests on the moral worth of the nation. We hope we are now coming to an end of a period when the assumption that targeting benefits through means-tests is both an effective mechanism for concentrating help on the poorest and an equally effective means of controlling public expenditure. Means-tests achieve neither objective. Social security has become disfigured by the spread of means-tests. In 1948, for each £10 paid in welfare, only £1 was means-tested. Now £1 in three is means tested. The Conservatives believe that cutting eligibility to both national insurance benefits and other non-means-tested assistance is an act of good housekeeping. Those losing benefits as a result of these curtailments are eligible for the means-tested safety net only if they have no other resources. As many people do have alternative sources of income, the Conservatives believe their strategy leads to significant public expenditure savings. That has been the belief. What has been the outcome in practice?

Looking at the figures alone might suggest their success here. Expenditure on national insurance benefit has risen since 1979 by 30 per cent. Expenditure on means-tests over the same period has soared by 300 per cent. That, the Tory Party might claim, was what was intended. But is it? For a party which used to be able to claim to have a firm grasp on human character, the Conservatives appear to misunderstand entirely how people are motivated.

Means-tests do not operate in the choice atmosphere of a House of Commons debate. Nor does social policy operate in a vacuum, particularly in respect of its interaction with our characters. Social policy can react on our individual motivation for either good or ill depending upon the balance of incentives and disincentives. Means-tests have a destructive impact.

Benefits are awarded on grounds of low income and savings. This indicates the likely impact on motivation. Means-tested benefits, which are progressively withdrawn as income rises, act as a penalty on work and effort. Similarly, as savings can disqualify a person from benefit, means-tests have a negative impact on savings levels, particularly of those most likely to qualify for help. As benefits can be kept only if income and savings are below the prescribed level, officials are deceived on income and savings. Means-tests thereby threaten honesty. The resentment caused either by the loss of benefit by remaining honest, or by what people see as their conscription into a nation on the make and who are willing to cheat, should not be underestimated.

It is here the Conservative Party stands doubly charged with naïvety. They have ignored the way means-test are eroding the values of work, effort, savings and honesty. How long can a society survive once these values are so determinedly undermined? Already one person in three lives in a household drawing one of the major means-tested benefits – double the number since 1979. But this naïvety about how human motivation will respond to incentives and disincentives is compounded by the Conservative expectation of how the spread of means-tests will help control the social security budget. Far from limiting claims, each £1 of means-tested benefit helps generate the next £1 claim of benefit. Once dishonesty has entered the system – as it now has on a massive scale – means-tests help perpetuate and expand claims.

The key assumption about social security take-up is that people stop claiming when their need ceases, i.e. when they are no longer unemployed or sick. But once people are claiming fraudulently, fraudulent claims do not usually come to a natural end until the fraud is exposed. And this pattern of fraudulent behaviour applies to individual claimants, to landlords and their agents, some of whom have turned housing benefit into a personal merchant bank, and groups of individuals who are best characterised as the new financial fraudsters. The Nick Leeson lesson needs to be learned in the DSS. In an age of computer-led fraud it is a great mistake to think of social security fraud only in terms of stolen giros, co-habitation, working on the side and drawing benefit and so on. These frauds are probably the most important in terms of individual fraudulent actions and the easiest to track down. But it is doubtful they now constitute the growth centre of fraud within the social security budget.

5: Social autonomy

This is not the end of the story – personal aspirations are changing. Part of the good life now is being able to set out and achieve this objective oneself. The means of obtaining the good life are becoming indistinguishable from the ends. This wish to do one's own thing shows up in the growing resistance to tax increases, which is of course a different stance from receiving more public goods at no extra tax cost. While current tax levels may be tolerated, tax increases which eat into current income levels, or further reduce expected income gains, strike at this new philosophy of prizing one's freedom to choose and to build one's own utopia.

Society is undergoing what I regard as a most fundamental change. In *How to Pay for the Future* I summed up this change with the phrase 'social autonomy'. People increasingly want to do their own thing – that part of the good life is not the securing of a set basket of goods and services, but deciding oneself on what and when to put objects into the basket. DIY in the home should be seen as the start of a total revolution which will have as much impact on our economic and political arrangements as it has on our social lives.

Accompanying this growing emphasis on the personal has

been a withdrawal from old fashioned collective efforts. By its very nature, collective provision denies people the choice and timing which is now increasingly becoming a premium. But this change is not a simple move back to nineteenth-century individualism. New ties are replacing the common endeavour. Family, friends and loved ones are the group within which individuals want to achieve the good life. Hence the phrase 'social autonomy'.

This tide should not be challenged. It is too strong. Opposition would be futile. So much of the change is good anyway and should not be opposed. It does, however, hold out a menacing danger for the poor. As greater numbers withdraw to do their own thing, a new pressure will grow on public services. The balance of power will move against those who continue to use the public sector, who will increasingly be the poorest, the least articulate and the least able. As more of the affluent leave the public domain, the pressure will mount for the curtailment of provision until a point is reached when public services disintegrate into a poor law service – thus compelling even more to quit its domain.

All these factors – an uncontrollable social security budget, the squeezing out of choice across the sweep of public expenditure, the destructive impact of means-tests on character, the resistance of voters and capital markets to increase taxation or borrowing and the establishment of social autonomy as a prime political force – are pushing against the status quo. Change is inevitable but where will it come from?

Direction of change

The direction is seen most clearly in the pensions field. Here two movements have been operating almost unobserved for some considerable time. First there is the disengagement from state welfare as the principal form of income maintenance. The steady movement into occupational pensions has come to an end. But the provision of what was so superiorly relegated into the category of occupational welfare has helped transform the retirement prospects of about half the work-force. As the occupational pension tide has faltered, its momentum has been garnered by the personal pension market. Despite all the adverse publicity about this form of pension savings, membership has soared. This is a simple but telling fact. It would appear that most buyers of personal pensions know they are being charged excessively for the sale and maintenance of their investment by the company which has purported to have sold them a personally crafted pension. Yet the sales continue to tumble in, and they do so despite FIMBRA's failure to bring to a satisfactory end the mis-selling scandal with the enforcement of adequate compensation rules. What would be the reaction out there in the market if there was a cheap and reliable form of pension savings, which also had all the important characteristics possessed by personal pensions, namely, individual ownership of the capital being accumulated?

One measure of the enthusiasm for the ownership of one's own pension, as opposed to membership of a state's scheme, comes from the stampede out of SERPS. And, despite all the knowledgeable guesses to the contrary by the grey beards, this headlong rush was overwhelmingly led by and composed of younger people. Of course personal ownership fits easily with the changes in a labour market where most individuals will have many jobs during their working lives.

This movement out of SERPS was not simply due to the opportunity to own one's pension capital, although that was clearly an element. It was also a reaction to a scheme where the writing had been etched onto the wall on more than one occasion. Benefit entitlement has been halved, only to be halved again. Anyone persuaded that SERPS has a future ought to be made a ward of court – there can be few more certain worse buys.

This disengagement has left the SERPS scheme mortally wounded. The scheme acts as a beacon, signalling the dangers awaiting state provision in an age where resistance to tax increases prevents radical improvement in benefit levels. The tide of membership recedes leaving behind many of the most poor and vulnerable. It is easy to decry such developments but it is much more important to consider what can be done.

One set of proposals – to rebuild SERPS – is, I believe, a non-starter. It is simply out of touch. There no longer exists the widespread trust for such a scheme and trust is only the first of a whole series of necessary ingredients for its success. The number of people who believe that taxpayers not yet born will pay the tax necessary to fund pensions for today's workers in a pay-as-you-go scheme is on the decline. Politically, this is not an option.

The crux issue

What should be done? Immediately we face what for me is the crux issue on welfare reform. The world is littered with countries reforming welfare, accepting a disengagement from monopoly state provision, encouraging different forms of private provision and casually allowing the bottom 20 per cent or so to sink into a segregated means-tested poor law type provision. Merely to follow in the wake of these developments would be to surrender Labour's heritage. If the party has stood for anything, it has been as a great force for an inclusive society. Here the equality of respect due to each of us is enshrined in our citizenship. And this citizenship is partly defined on the basis of welfare provision, to which each of us earns our entitlement, and will become ever more so if the stakeholder concept is realised in the reform of welfare.

How that provision is provided is, I believe, a secondary issue – whether it comes from the state, private or mutual aid sources – to this fundamental point. Later, I argue for the role of mutual aid provision. But even here, and despite the many attractions mutual aid has in strengthening those civilised values which I believe to be of vital importance, the end goal of inclusiveness is by far and away the major objective. Indeed without this, those other values which I associate as thriving by-products of mutual aid will themselves be stunted and limited.

To invert the traditional catechismal definition of a sacrament, and refashion it into a political aspiration, the inward meaning of equality is given an outward expression in welfare's incorporation. That incorporation can only come from combining a system of compulsory membership with personal ownership of the welfare capital which results. This is one additional but vital consideration. There will need to be an element of financial transfer to the poorest outside the labour market, and to those who are low paid, so that their contributions are met and inclusiveness thereby gained. I would argue, however, that this redistribution – a word which radicals should not be afraid to use – needs to be above board, to be clearly of a targeted form, to be made and agreed by taxpayers as a whole, financed by the Exchequer and on no account paid for by means of a surreptitious filching of funds from individual scheme-holders' accounts.

This takes us now to the important but secondary consideration of how this universal benefit will be supplied. Here I depart from the traditional Left thinking in welcoming a multiplicity of suppliers. I do so because I believe choice is thankfully going to become more and not less important to voters, and that while choice always holds dangers, such drawbacks are less than the advantages which come when the entrepreneurial spirit encounters unmet demand. Choice is not, as some of the Left see it, a danger against which it should rail. Rather it should be welcomed for what it is, and also for the opportunity it offers to advance our own values, some of which are enshrined in the mutual aid principle. Let us return to the argument on pension reform.

New savings vehicles

The details of a phasing in of a compulsory universal scheme of funded pensions was given in *Making Welfare Work*, and the transitional programme to that end is fleshed out in *How to Pay for the Future*.[3] The demand for simple long-term savings vehicles is the issue on which we need to concentrate here. It will come from two sources. One will be those brought into the scheme of funded pensions for the first time. But there will be a larger demand from those already in a personal pension scheme, who realised from the start what a poor buy it was, that it was Hobson's choice, that it was the best option available under the restricted circumstances of the time, but who will be looking to transfer their savings to a more economical vehicle once the opportunity arises. The ground rules for transferring will have to be considered very carefully by parliament. The aim will be to strengthen the hand of the individual against unwarranted and penal costs imposed by pension companies against those wishing to transfer. The private sector will understandably scream blue murder – or will it be red? – on this point. But this is not a new issue. Under occupational pension schemes, early leavers were wickedly penalised, and change was forced on the schemes by parliament. So too with private pension provision. It will be a test for a Blair government to show that it is capable of standing up to not only vested interests on its own side, but vested interests wherever they reside. The commitment of the government should be to protect the individual against the corporate vested interest whenever there is a conflict.

One of the criticisms made about the proposal for universal second pension provision I outlined in *Making Welfare Work* (to run alongside the existing national insurance retirement pension) has centred on the recommendation that these contributions should be compulsory. These critics fail to appreciate that there is already a compulsory contribution required for second pension coverage from every worker whose income is above the lower earnings level for national insurance contribution purposes. In *Making Welfare Work* I argued only for a modification of this policy. The suggestion was, first, to bring all workers in, no matter how small their earnings might be in any one year. The second modification was to close the pay-as-you-go SERPS scheme and redirect these SERPS contributions into funded schemes chosen by the contributors themselves. These subsidies to low wage earners for their contributions, and the coverage of pension contributions for those outside the labour market, together with the costs of meeting SERPS entitlements already earned, are set out in my paper *How to Pay for the Future*.

What should be at the centre of the debate is the form of savings vehicles which will be on offer to attract these new savings and, I believe, much more important in terms of size, the capital already being saved which will become footloose under the reform which allows individuals to disengage themselves from existing high cost personal pension schemes. Freedom will be the essence. The private sector will be able to compete for these savings. But against them raising the stakes, will be the mutual aid players. Charges will tumble on two counts. One will be the fierceness of the competition. With the advent of compulsion for funded schemes the defence of high charges – large sale forces are necessary to attract the money of unwilling savers – is knocked away. Firms will therefore be forced to attempt to attract trade by the scale of their charges. And the sales emphasis should be at this point rather than the bogus figures on likely returns on investment. Indeed the publication of such data should be prohibited. But the mutual aid component will add a new cutting edge to these competitive forces.

Mutual aid organisations are membership bodies which build over many decades a collectively owned business. They are commercially orientated organisations, as concerned at providing as effective service to the customer/investor as any privately owned body or public company. The vital difference is that in mutual aid bodies there is no group of shareholders to whom dividends are paid. Surpluses are ploughed back into the organisation through lower premiums, or more generous benefits or a combination of both.

Mutual aid fightback

Here then is another paradox in an area littered with paradoxical circumstances. A case is being unfolded for a major advance in the operation of mutual aid at the very time when more and more mutual aid companies are being stalked by predators or attacked from within by their boards proposing a change in status to public companies. The capital of a mutually owned company has been built up over time with the membership of any one generation receiving the value added by past members, usually adding to that value themselves, and handing the enhanced capital on to the next generation. The drive to public company status is destroying this inter-generational trusteeship.

Abbey National led the way. The main value of the capital which had been owned mutually did not go to the then current membership, but was largely gained by the new private owners. It was for this very objective that Abbey National was bought out of its mutually aided status. The sad tale is that it is from these very bodies, where the past commitment to mutual aid has been most generously expressed, that the most succulent victims to the private sector predator are presented. Greater safeguards are needed so that mutual aid companies are not picked off unfairly by private sector predators.

There is also the need for the mutual aid organisations themselves to become proactive in defence of bodies under attack. Why should these take-overs be left to the private sector? If the gain in the value of the capital, goodwill and future prospects are attractive to the private sector, why are other mutual aid companies not entering into the fray and bidding for this capital? Even the more aggressive policy of bodies like Northern Rock, where cuts in mortgage rates and higher savings rates are attempting to bolster still further member loyalty, constitutes only a defensive strategy. We have yet to see the mutual aid bodies going on to the attack in defence of their domain.

Mutual aid's political agenda
The new era of universal compulsory pension contributions

to funded schemes offers the chance to rebuild, extending and creating new mutual aid organisations. I do not have the space here to consider the details of these savings schemes. Instead I want to spell out the attractiveness of the mutual aid principle to this area and to consider how a future radical government might ensure that the voice of these bodies is kept above the hubbub of the selling campaign which will rightly be raised by private sector companies.

The attraction of mutual aid organisations to centre left politics is such that it is a puzzle why it has not registered more strongly in the current situation. One explanation must be that the period of statist solutions was so total it had a numbing effect on the creation of alternative ways of providing universal services. Whereas the Blair revolution has thrown over this hegemony, it has yet to rediscover Labour's past and begin prizing those key values which set in motion the beginnings of the socialist commonwealth. These were commonwealths which were not simply dreams which disappear with daybreak. They were and are a reality. Moreover, the reality was not one organised by central bureaucracies, but by the members themselves almost invariably in locally or regionally based groups. Here there was no need to talk of community. Here was the community.

And what was the basis of the flowering of these little, and after a time not so little, mutual aid commonwealths? First, their actions were based on beliefs which are far from inappropriate today. The starting point was simple, namely, that acting alone an individual might achieve some gains, but nothing compared to what was possible if those very same individuals worked together. So mutual aid began to change lives – through building societies, co-operatives, friendly societies, savings banks, public libraries and mutual life insurance – long before trade unions became a force, and even before parliamentary representation was achieved. Members pooled their resources so homes could be bought – sometimes building them – the quality of food and clothes and household goods were raised through the retail and wholesale co-operatives, and the vagaries of economic life were guarded against through friendly society protection.

Mutual aid both valued and kept in balance self-interest – that most powerful of human motivations – directing it in such a way that the common interest was simultaneously advanced. Indeed much of its attraction to members must have been that self-interest could only be advanced as part of a collective endeavour. One could not have a better example of the one strengthening the other. Mutual aid stands in counter-position to the crudities of Thatcherism where only self-interest was valued. It similarly contrasts with Old Labour and its unhealthy and unsustainable emphasis on the primacy of altruism in public policy.

The mutual aid movement was not divorced from another of the social objectives of the Victorian period. The emphasis on character, its safeguarding and its advance, was not an idiosyncratic concern of the Charity Organisation Society and similar bodies, no matter how the uninformed Left try to suggest otherwise today. Here was a belief which spread beyond upper-middle-class reformers and which was very much part of working-class culture and aspiration. The mutual aid movement cannot be understood without a proper appreciation of the importance given to the idea of self-improvement. Mankind was thought of in terms of a bundle of abilities and motives with potential which could be developed for good or ill. The mutual aid movement held out the prospect of an organisational form through which members were able to advance their independence and gain control over the vagaries of life – of the ever present prospect of being engulfed in poverty, pauperism and the poor law, and of safeguarding themselves and their families from the destructive force excessive drink brought in its wake. Above all it was the means by which *de facto* citizenship was attained. 'We might be working class but our behaviour is equal if not superior to any other class', was the proud cry of those who peopled these mutual aid organisations. Indeed, once these self-governing organisations began to transform working-class life on what basis could the franchise be refused? The franchise reforms were merely a public recognition of the citizenship which had already been established by friendly society and mutual aid activities and actions.

The responsibility for self-improvement was clearly located. It rested with individuals themselves, although it was sought through co-operative effort. So again our forebears have a crucial lesson for us about how successful social advance is gained. The individual was not demeaned as he or she is by so much of today's left-wing ideology which puts all the emphasis on structural causes as the reasons for preventing personal advance. But neither was it naïve in believing that the structural forces were without importance. Again a proper sense of balance of both these arguments was, I believe, achieved.

Labour's new agenda

How should a Labour government advance the idea of
mutual aid? Labour should publish a statement on
democratic socialist values which elevates mutual aid to its
proper position in the scheme of things. The much quoted
values of liberty, equality and fraternity should be seen as
advancing through the promotion of mutual aid operations.
Mutual aid should be seen as the catalyst for transforming
welfare and this does not have to wait for a Labour
government. Indeed the spelling out of such an approach
may help to ensure that election victory.

This statement of values should be followed by the
Labour Party beginning detailed discussions with the mutual
aid movement on its role in welfare reform. What is
proposed is to give the mutual aid movement the maximum
amount of time to plan and organise how it will capitalise on
a Labour commitment to universalise funded pension
provision. How can existing mutual aid companies expand?
How can new mutual aid bodies, organised on an industry-
wide basis, trade or professional, by local authorities or trade
unions, on a local or a regional basis, be encouraged? The
Labour leadership should not only begin these discussions,
but also propose to publish a joint strategy paper outlining
what action could be agreed before an election and then, in
the build up to the publication of a series of social security
bills which will be needed in the next parliament, what
further action mutual aid organisations could take while
these bills, after being published, are publicly discussed, and

then moved through their parliamentary stages. From publication of the first bill to Royal Assent will probably take two years. So in all three years is offered for planning a mutual aid renaissance.

The most radical members of the mutual aid movement are already putting forward sweeping evolutionary changes which would transform the whole of current welfare provision. Their aim is for a three-tier welfare state: a state guaranteed minimum, the compulsory purchase of a comprehensive policy covering all main social security needs and voluntary membership of top-up additional insurance coverage. At the very minimum Labour needs to consider these proposals carefully. A 'no reform' stance will deliver up today's welfare to the constant war of attrition being waged by a much enlivened private sector. The voters at the very least deserve to have an alternative to this scenario.

I hope I have provided an outline of what that alternative could be. Mutual aid is not an idea which lives only in the museum of political ideas. It is one which draws deep on the roots of Labour and radical politics, which themselves have always reflected a profound understanding of human nature and the means of human advance. That conception of human nature has been one which has easily accepted the primacy of self-interest as the greatest motive in practically all of us. But mutual aid has by its very nature channelled this power of self-interest into a great engine force for self-improvement. It is the idea that self-improvement is *the* goal of social policy which needs to be reasserted and acted upon. We live in an age when the nation state's writ no longer reflects the world's economic power structure. Facing undaunted the unbridled power of laissez-faire capitalism, our ancestors quietly brought self-interest and self-improvement together and showed that by a common endeavour the deeply hostile world could be tamed. We need a similar vision and programme of action today.

7: The High Politics of Welfare

Attlee Lecture,[36] February 12th 1996

The importance of welfare in the political debate has varied dramatically over the last two centuries. The early Victorian political settlement neutralised what many of us would have regarded as normal day to day political activity. The repeal of the Corn Laws and the passing of the Bank Charter Act took most commercial and monetary questions out of party debate. The implementation of the new Poor Law similarly settled social policy. The impact of these measures on the political process can be misread. While the big issues were not subject to party political dispute and division, they were not entirely taken out of politics. The very basis of the political settlement was that the commanding heights of the political economy should not be questioned, let alone overturned.

Hence the radicalism of Joe Chamberlain. His Unauthorised Programme doubly holed this status quo below its waterline. The Peelite view that opposition should not put forward a programme until they had been 'called in' was directly confronted. One of the great fears of the political élite, that in the age of an extending franchise politicians would start bidding for the popular vote, was refashioned by Chamberlain into a radical virtue. And following hard on the heels of this challenge came another Chamberlain broadside. Fiscal issues ceased to be a matter of raising the necessary revenue with the minimum disturbance to private interests. Redistribution entered into the political fray. Welfare was again set on course for high politics.

This was a challenge which Gladstone appeared only too anxious to counter. He excluded Chamberlain from the government's inner circle and rejected his Unofficial

Programme and with it a new wave of radicalism. And his drive to a new constitutional settlement with the Irish played a pivotal part in the breakup of the old Liberal Party and its exclusion from power for almost twenty years. A new radical settlement had to wait for the Liberal landslide of 1906 and the use to which Lloyd George and Churchill put this overwhelming parliamentary majority. The high politics of that time was seen as a search by New Liberalism to forge a sustaining coalition of voters.

Welfare is set once again to become the issue of high politics. A new political settlement is falling into place over the political landscape. The collapse of the Berlin Wall, and the cross-party agreement on the priority given to controlling inflation, has largely removed foreign affairs and the running of the economy from the day to day battle of party politics. Welfare is sucked into the centre of this party political vacuum. It has moved into the centre of politics for a number of other reasons too.

It would command that central position on matters of finance alone. Throughout the post-war period the size of the welfare budget has not merely increased but, at a time when the overall size of the government budget has itself grown, welfare has risen both in real terms and as a percentage of GDP. To develop Sir Geoffrey Holland's graphic phrase, welfare now holds such a dominant position in the government finances that public expenditure questions are for other departments matters of scavenging the scraps from welfare's feast.

Moreover, the cost of this feast is out of control. The Conservative Party has been committed to a programme of reining back the rate of increase in welfare expenditure. Despite strengthening the excluding powers of the gatekeepers guarding the entrance to welfare's domain, and the sending in of official raiding parties to expel many of those already in residence, the welfare army continues to expand. And so too do the costs.

In the last four annual public expenditure rounds the welfare budget's projected total has been increased each year, only for this projected increase to be overrun by at least £1,000 million, for that projected total to be increased again, and to be overrun by at least £1,000 million again and so on. Even if a Labour government fires successfully on all its other policy cylinders, this uncontrollable welfare budget would immediately prevent the government from ordering its priorities between, say, education, transport, overseas aid, health and so on. The lion's share of any increase in expenditure allowed from a growing economy would be forfeited to social security without discussion. But, given welfare's insatiable appetite, the process would not stop there. Merely to project the current growth of welfare as part of government expenditure is to recognise that the spectre of it derailing the government's overall strategy is a distinct possibility. Controlling welfare expenditure must become the cornerstone of Labour's domestic policy.

But welfare becomes high politics for another, equally important reason. Let us ignore for a moment the question of who picks up the tab. The image of welfare was that this expenditure was beneficial to the recipient. It is this view which must now be brought into the frame. Far from having a clear beneficial impact, the fastest growing part of the welfare budget is insidiously undermining the moral fabric of our society.

Expenditure on means-tested welfare is growing out of control. National insurance benefit expenditure has risen by 30 per cent since 1979. Means-tested benefit costs have soared by 300 per cent. It is this particular expenditure which is playing such a part in destabilising the overall budget. Much of each pound expenditure on means-tests generates the next pound of welfare expenditure.

The reason for this is disarmingly simple. Yet its essential simplicity has escaped the Conservatives' understanding; a fact which is itself doubly surprising. Here is a political party with a not inconsiderable amount of intellectual ability, despite much evidence to the contrary. The talents, for example, of Peter Lilley are of the first order. And yet the Conservative Party seems to have so moved from its traditional moorings that it now fails to appreciate the impact of means-tested welfare on human character. Having an accurate view of human nature used to be the starting point for all Tory policies, and a clear dividing line with Labour, who allegedly held a distorted, too idealistic view of the human condition.

Any rational society would arrange its affairs so that those values which it believes central to the good life are not merely protected, but actively promoted. Means-tested welfare achieves precisely the opposite. Means-tests set an operational framework within which the cardinal values of work, saving and honesty attract extreme financial penalties. Men and women are more rational economic animals than even Mrs Thatcher cared to consider. Self-interest is the paramount force driving each of us. This self-interest operates within a framework of long-set traditions and the immediate pressures of current laws, entitlements and penalties. Means-tests set self-interest against society's overall welfare. Means-tested welfare penalises work, or working harder, makes the provision of additional income from sources like company or private pensions a foolhardy venture, particularly if those pensions are of modest amounts, disenfranchises from benefit those who have saved and denies help to many who answer income and savings questions honestly. Simply reining back the hold means-tests have is not the only subject that matters to welfare's reconstruction, although it is the most immediate. Self-interest has to be given the opportunity to promote the common good, and how that objective can be achieved is an issue which I shall discuss later.

How can welfare be reconstructed in a way which achieves a disengagement from means-tests? The answer to this question bears directly on welfare's financial crisis. In *Making Welfare Work*, I proposed three new initiatives to achieve this objective. The first was to universalise funded pension provision which would then run alongside the state's retirement pension. Stakeholding here will stem from the ownership of the savings in the funded scheme. The second reform centres on establishing a new national insurance system where the stakeholders are in control. It is crucial that these reforms are set in place even though they will not have an immediate impact on the welfare budget. The third reform, turning Income Support from a passive into a proactive agency, will have the most immediate impact on welfare bills while simultaneously offering real possibilities for claimants to free themselves legitimately from dependency.

This threefold welfare reconstruction programme must be seen as having fundamentally different effects at different times on the welfare budget. Pension reform is crucial. More than any other reform it offers the chance to usher in the new stakeholder welfare society which I first advocated in *Making Welfare Work*. But it does nothing to ease the immediate financial crisis. Pension reform is about creating the conditions in which those voters who currently make inadequate savings increase their amount of savings from current income so that retirement income levels become adequate. Full implementation of the reform outlined in *Making Welfare Work* will not affect the apparently inexorable rise in the cost of today's welfare by a single penny. Indeed, if the universalism of these proposals is accepted, helping the poorest make their pension contributions – and this is the crucial distinguishing mark from anything that will be offered by the Tories – means the bill will actually be increased.

The proposal for universal funded pensions is about facing the cruel truth that, in an age of growing tax cut demands, *more* not *less* must be spent on welfare. We should not be beguiled by Peter Lilley's rhetoric. Retirement incomes are the most obvious area where this is true and the easiest to confront. It takes only a moment's thought to see that if individuals work for fewer years, but live for more decades in retirement, an adequate income for these decades can only be achieved if more of today's earnings are set aside for later consumption. But I do not believe that this transfer will be agreed unless the welfare rules are totally changed. Individual savers will want individual ownership of their assets. And who can blame them? By putting this reform into place, welfare expenditure increases but state welfare in time will decline. But while the total welfare expenditure would increase, the increase will not go through the Exchequer. Nor will it be seen as part of the government's accounts. The increase will all safely be in individual hands and individual ownership.

Even the proposals for establishing a Stakeholder National Insurance Scheme – to run in the first instance a new system of unemployment insurance, as well as a care pension – will cost some additional funding. The ownership of this scheme will need to pass from the government to the contributors. The reason for this is quite simple. We only have to look at what has happened to national insurance unemployment benefit rights to understand why this change is necessary. First, the earnings related supplements were abolished. Then the Conservative government tightened the qualifications for benefit. Finally the twelve month right to benefit is slashed in half by the Tories as part of their Jobseeker Allowance reform. There will be savings to taxpayers as the transition from means-tested dependency for the households of the unemployed takes effect, and the whole strategy of community care funding will be fundamentally changed. These savings will be dramatic in more than one sense. Savings will be dramatic because the cost of means-tested welfare will fall. The change to the Stakeholder's National Insurance Scheme will have equally dramatic consequences as the impact of welfare on motivation and character will be so clearly seen that only the political dinosaurs hankering after the old order will fail to recognise the obvious. The proposals for a new stakeholder's national insurance scheme, which was first outlined in *Making Welfare Work* and will be detailed and costed in *How to Pay for the Future,* advocates restructuring unemployment benefit to accommodate modern conditions. Let me give a few more details of this reform as it illustrates how a stakeholder's welfare has to be built in order to complement today's labour market.

In 1979 those re-entering the labour market were most likely to come from households where no-one was in work. Today the position is totally the reverse. Why? There are two reasons for this phenomenal change which give the clearest illustration imaginable of how current welfare inter-relates with the labour market – this time creating horrendous consequences for both individuals and families as well as for taxpayers.

First, since 1979 the wages paid to re-entry jobs have collapsed. Almost half of the jobs which go to those re-entering work pay less than a quarter of median earnings: i.e. below £56 per week. Second, consider the benefit system. Unemployment benefit is paid for twelve months but this is to be cut to six. During this time a wage earner picks up £48.25 a week without questions being asked about a partner's earnings. The search is therefore for a job which pays above, and hopefully well above, the benefit level. Now consider what happens when there is no insurance benefit. A means-tested income is only offered after taking into account the partner's earnings. The benefit income of £150 or above from income support and housing benefit is more than the income most partners would gain from work. Pound for pound is deducted from any of those earnings except for a miserly disregarded amount. The outcome is obvious. The partner gives up work too. It pays to do so. But once out of work what chance is there of either partner finding a job paying more than benefit? Given that most re-entry jobs pay below £56 a week, we have the basis of the work/no-work households. It will be made much worse as the new Jobseeker's Allowance cuts unemployment benefit entitlement from twelve to six months.

How to Pay for the Future lays down the basis for a stakeholder's national insurance scheme where those taking re-entry jobs, which often have a short shelf-life, are rewarded for so doing. They will quickly requalify for insurance benefit. Risk-taking is therefore rewarded. Families are kept off means-tests. Long-term dependency is countered rather than encouraged by the benefit system. Work is more evenly spread throughout the community. Household income thereby becomes more equitable and a start is made simultaneously in closing the widening income gap which has so disfigured Britain, particularly since 1979. The National Insurance Stakeholder reform sets the scene for curtailing the spread and then for the reduction in means-tested welfare. But the savings from this approach will be gained only in the longer term.

Dealing with the immediate financial crisis and welfare's dependency culture puts means-tested income support as the central issue. Indeed the financial crisis, and the spread of the dependency culture are, as I have already argued, intimately linked. A government wishing to roll back this culture, and a Labour chancellor anxious to prevent the welfare budget from imploding, has to consider the means-tested income support welfare budget if the current position is to be not just tinkered with, but radically altered. Moreover, if welfare's bill is to be controlled, and if a higher proportion of its monies are to be spent encouraging values which the wider electorate supports, an attack on the dependency culture about which the Conservatives so hotly rail, while simultaneously spreading that very culture over greater and greater numbers of people, is essential. How can these objectives be achieved?

In *Making Welfare Work* I argued for a simple but revolutionary approach. The plea was for a rejection of the whole strategy which has dominated the poverty agenda ever since the mid-1960s. Since the early years of the Wilson government the approach has been to devise programmes for helping particular groups of the poor, first by designating very poor areas for priority in government funding, then by singling out particular groups of the poor, such as the unemployed or single parents, and lastly, targeting only sub-groups, i.e. those who are unemployed for over two years.

As the policy objectives have narrowed, so too have the criteria for what makes a successful reform. The debate, instead of concentrating and advancing first principles, has collapsed into a near obsession with fine tuning the regulations governing entitlement, offering a little incentive here, building a disincentive there. A comparison with the First World War is apposite. When war was declared in August 1914, the expectation was for a quick sweep through

France, then on to Berlin, with the troops returning home by Christmas. It was not long before this grand strategy became bogged down in the mud of Flanders' fields. Conservative government ministers look increasingly like those First World War generals whose vision collapsed into a mere obsession over gaining or regaining the next trench. Progress was tortuously slow and the expense unjustifiable. So too with this country's anti-poverty strategy. The whole effort is directed to fine tuning without casting a glance at impacts the various programmes are having on human nature and the motivation both of those groups targeted by reform and, equally importantly, of those who are excluded.

Moreover, all these modern anti-poverty programmes share a further characteristic. They aim at doing good to the poor. They do not seek to liberate the poor. They aim to control the actions of the targeted group and, consequently, only a limited range of options are offered. This conventional wisdom about how best to help the poor should be opposed, not only because it patently has not worked, but also, quite simply, because it no longer meets the challenge. The long-term changes in the distribution of income has had the effect of kicking more and more people down to the bottom of society, and for those at the bottom the prospect of destitution is once again a real possibility. From time immemorial the beggar was part of British life. The first legislation to tackle the problem appeared under Elizabeth I. Begging became extinct during Mr Attlee's stewardship, only to return again under Mrs Thatcher. Today's anti-poverty strategy, whose roots go back to the 1960s, no longer offers the chance of succeeding in an age of mass pauperisation.

But this is not all. There is worse to come. The form of help offered is now part of the problem, not part of its solution. The numbers on means-tested welfare grow inexorably. Each means-tested claim helps feed the next. Means-tests interact in a perverse and pernicious way on human motivation and thereby on character. Any imaginable welfare state will need a means-tested safety net acting in a limited manner for those without income from work, wealth or insurance entitlement. That was the role sensibly envisaged by the Attlee government for means-tests. But that emphatically is not what we are faced with today. Let us consider the three main means-tests – income support, housing benefit and family credit. A third of the entire population lives in households drawing one of these means-tested benefits – an unsustainable proportion which has doubled since 1979, and is still growing.

The crisis we face is urgent. The hour is late. A dramatic initiative is required which aims not to undermine the growing army of the poor still further but quite simply to change the political culture in which welfare operates. Moreover, the strategy must offer hope to the many rather than the few.

The issue immediately arises of what kind of strategy needs to be adopted if this dual crisis – of finance and dependency – is to be countered. Up until now, all attempts at reform have been piecemeal, targeted efforts. The continuation of such an approach must be resisted. I am not, however, making an appeal for a 'big bang' solution. After the Child Support Agency fiasco I simply do not have the courage or the foolhardiness to do so. The CSA fiasco has understandably undermined the confidence of reformers. Rather I am advocating a strategy which reverses the traditional approach. Instead of singling out particular groups of claimants, and doing good to them, the reform is devastatingly simple. Its aim is quite simply to set the claimants free. In 1976, I argued for the mass sale of council houses, that this should be Labour's policy, and that this policy should specifically be presented in terms of freeing the millions of tenants from the serfdom imposed upon them by autocratic local authorities. I now make the same plea for income support claimants. It is time similarly to free them from the bondage of the Poor Law dependency which excludes them from the labour market. Such a programme would turn millions of claimants into a great engine force against the growing culture of dependency.

My paper *Making Welfare Work* outlined such an approach. The proposal was not a national programme offering help to single parents or the unemployed. It offered the opportunity to all claimants to escape means-tested dependency. It is nothing less than a turning of income support from a passive into a proactive agency. Even as a passive agency income support does not score very highly. The Comptroller and Auditor General has qualified the accounts each year since the scheme came into existence. The Agency has two tasks: to pay benefit and to check on fraud, neither of which it does with much finesse. The Comptroller's last report puts the error rate at over 16 per cent for the payment of benefit. In addition fraud is detected in one in ten claims.

Even worse than this pretty abysmal record is the fact that income support can only be paid if claimants remain idle.

There are cases where this rule does not apply – the disregarded sums for those with other income, for example. But the latest figures show that most of this disregarded income is claimed by pensioners, and not by those of working age. So these exceptions make little difference to the tenor of the organisation. It fulfils the main objective of the old Poor Law. Those now requiring help do not have to enter the workhouse. But an equally telling exclusion is insisted upon. Generally speaking these individuals are excluded from the labour market. It is easy to understand that such a policy might be unthinkingly adopted in the early post-war period when overwhelmingly it was pensioners who sought help from the then National Assistance Board. That is no longer the case, and has not been so for almost two decades. Today, for every pensioner on income support, there are almost five other claimants of non-pensionable age.

In *Making Welfare Work*, I proposed a fundamental reordering of income support, its objectives and the delivery of its benefits for those below pensionable age. The idea that income support should be paid while people await a return to the labour market is no longer appropriate – nor is it a desirable objective in an age of widespread fraud. Breaks in employment are, for all too many, no short spell of idleness, but a condemnation to a long-term exclusion from the labour market.

I proposed that every claimant below pensionable age and fit for work would be expected to plan for what they want to do and achieve during the rest of their working lives. Everyone would be concerned with drawing up a career or life plan. All too many of my constituents have never been accorded the dignity of being asked simple questions about their hopes and wishes for the future, let alone how they might go about achieving such goals. They therefore have no sense of a goal, a general direction or of any official support in achieving anything.

Of course, the scheme could not immediately be brought into universal effect. It would have to be phased in. I have suggested in *How to Pay for the Future* how this plan will work, starting with those aged under twenty-six. This is the group which gains a lower rate of benefit. Even so, I judge the take-up rate will be such that local staff, whose skills will have to be extended to make the reform effective and combined with the expertise of their job centre colleagues, will be overwhelmed with takers. Income support will be used as an educational maintenance allowance for those going on training courses to help them achieve their career objectives. It will, of course, be necessary to limit further this scheme to those aged under twenty-six who have been on benefit for two years. Otherwise there is the danger of the Filofax families tipping their offspring onto income support to ensure that all the stages of further education are paid for by income support grants.

It will also be necessary to link in one further reform. Student grants should be converted into universal loans, run by the private sector, with the sums being clawed back through the tax system. The £1.1 billion thereby released will be used to expand nursery education and child care facilities. There will be no additional revenue costs, but parents on benefit will have the chance of fully participating in the income support liberation programme.

This enfranchising measure will simultaneously achieve a number of key objectives. It will signify that:

- the old system of income support is coming to an end
- a large part of the dead cost of welfare's budget will be turned into an investment budget
- claimants will have both an opportunity and a duty to build their own life rafts from dependency
- genuine claimants are liberated by this reform while at the same time acting as an effective check on fraud.

Allowing claimants to devise their own exits from benefit transforms the millions who are currently relegated to being mere onlookers to their own fate, into an army of activists in the battle against dependency. For that will be the inevitable outcome of allowing individuals the chance to use their benefit payments as training and educational investment allowances. No policy maker, however clever, has the technical knowledge or the brain power equal to those millions who are currently condemned to stand on the sidelines while Britain struggles to reorder itself. This is the extent of the force which waits to be reincentivised.

Claimants invited to discuss their career plans should know that an amnesty operates for those who admit that they do not need a career plan for the very simple reason that they are already fully occupied and working. If an amnesty can be given for those returning dangerous knives, one can surely be offered in this war on income support fraud, thereby drawing a line under the problem.

The reform would also have a major impact on the level of fraud against the DSS. The Comptroller and Auditor General's figure of fraud in one in ten claims, cited earlier, is, I believe, an underestimate. It is against a proper realisation of the extent of fraud that changes in the running of the DSS must be viewed. The Conservatives' decision to phase out routine home visits had a doubly damaging effect on the efficient running of the Department. Officials involved in visiting claimants in their own homes were able to advise claimants, often pensioners, on their full entitlements. Officers returning to base after such visits would also give fraud officers much information about following up suspected fraud which they had gained only because they had undertaken detailed visits to particular localities.

The Tories are now considering introducing self-assessment for some benefits. One wonders what world they are living in. It has proved impossible for them to deal effectively with fraud where claimants are required to produce corroborative evidence supporting their claim. The Department is now planning to invite people to make their own claims for benefit. Such a scheme might have worked in the Garden of Eden. It certainly has no place in the rough and tumble of our fraud-ridden world.

It is here that the proposal to change Income Support from a passive to a proactive agency is important. The reform offers real opportunities to claimants planning the next stages of their lives. It will simultaneously act as a massive check on fraud. Since this proposal for a proactive agency was made in *Making Welfare Work* the Social Security Select Committee made a visit to New Zealand to study their pension arrangements. What the Committee found was a reform almost identical to that proposed in *Making Welfare Work* already in operation. Three consequences were very apparent:

1. Large numbers of claimants had freed themselves from benefit and into work.
2. Over two hundred suggestions from staff for further reforms of the social security system have been put into operation.
3. Large numbers of claimants when invited for an interview to plan their careers admitted they needed no such plan as they were already in work. This group then left the welfare roll under amnesty arrangements.

The same results I believe would result in Britain if these proposals for an active agency were implemented. Amnesties should be offered to all those coming forward to close a fraudulent social security account. We would find here that, as in New Zealand, the actual social security budget began to fall – not as a slowdown in the rate of increase which is all politicians have so far offered – but by an actual decrease in the budget in money terms. That will be achieved simultaneously with offering claimants the opportunity to plan their own lives. If these plans became effective further cuts in the welfare budget would then naturally result.

Attlee's welfare settlement is being transformed and once again this area becomes the high politics of our time. In this lecture I have argued that three inter-related reforms are urgent. Clear red or blue water – depending upon which ship one is in – should emerge over pension reform. Will Labour move to make second funded pensions compulsory? Such a move would enshrine the Attlee principle of universality and inclusiveness, but would also apply the reform through the private and mutual aid sectors. Failure to embrace compulsion will leave little difference between the Tory strategy and that which Labour intends to adopt. Only by universalising will the stakeholder as an inclusive concept become valid.

A second reform concerns establishing a stakeholder national insurance scheme. Here I have argued that the reform should be introduced so that it deals first with unemployment and the introduction of a new care pension. Again, as with pension reform, this change will require increases in income allocated to welfare, although the increases will be controlled by the contributors, and to some extent they will be matched by cuts in taxation as the new insurance schemes take effect.

It is in the third reform, of converting the passive income support into a proactive agency, that the largest changes will occur, both in the opportunities offered to the poor, and in saving very substantial sums of taxpayers' money. As mentioned earlier, the plea here is one which matches the scale and change brought about by the sale of council houses. Put simply, it is about setting claimants free, allowing them to use their income support payments to build their own life rafts from dependency back into the labour market. I have argued that such a reform will be as effective in controlling fraud as it will be in offering freedom from the Poor Law culture of inactivity imposed on millions of income support claimants.

Notes and references

1 Alan Deacon, *Stakeholder Welfare*, IEA, 1977.

2 Frank Field, *Making Welfare Work*, Institute of Community Studies, 1995.

3 Frank Field, *How to Pay for the Future*, Institute of Community Studies, 1995.

4 David Marquand and Anthony Seldon (eds.), *The Ideas That Shape Post-War Britain*, Fontana, 1977.

5 Ibid. p. 20.

6 Peter Clarke, *Liberals and Social Democrats*, Cambridge University Press, 1978.

7 Raymond Plant, 'Social Democracy' in Marquand and Seldon (eds.), op. cit.

8 Ibid. p. 173.

9 Ibid. pp. 173–74.

10 Alan Deacon, *Self-interest and Collective Welfare*, paper presented at Edinburgh University, pp. 22–23.

11 I do, of course, accept that, as far as policy goes, as opposed to principles, there can be no permanent, long-term, sustainable political *status quo*. The very nature of human existence precludes such an outcome. But there can be success for a period of time, hence my emphasis on the *longer* run.

12 Marquand, in Marquand and Seldon (eds.), op. cit. p. 27.

13 Ibid. pp. 26–27.

14 Alan Deacon, *Stakeholder Welfare*, op. cit.

15 Noel Annan, *Leslie Stephen: The Godless Victorian*, Weidenfeld and Nicolson, 1984.

16 Andrew Vincent and Raymond Plant, *Philosophy, Politics and Citizenship: The Life and Thoughts of the British Idealists*, Basil Blackwell, 1984.

17 The state pension constitutes 85% of income of the poorest 10% of pensioners.

18 It is true that the army of carers goes well beyond the group defined by the ICA, but this does not affect the principle I am arguing.

19 A.M.McBriar, *An Edwardian Mixed Doubles*, McClarendon Press, 1987.

20 Deacon, *Stakeholder Welfare*, op. cit. pp.18–19.

21 Ibid. cited p. 12.

22 Frank Field, *Welfare: New Labour Markets and Fiscal Reform*, Institute of Directors Annual Lecture, February 27th 1997. Published here as Chapter 4.

23 Frank Field, *Rebuilding Mutual Aid*, a speech to the UK Co-operative Council, Fifth Annual Forum, Manchester, November 22nd 1996. Published here as Chapter 5.

24 Alan Deacon, letter dated May 19th 1997.

25 Deacon, *Stakeholder Welfare*, op. cit. p. 14.

26 Ibid. p. 17.

27 Ibid. p. 17.

28 See the portrait painted by his daughter, Ann Oakley, of her parents' marriage in *Man and Wife*, HarperCollins, 1996.

29 Frank Field, *Do We Need Council Houses?*, CHAS, 1976.

30 It is of course proper for groups to promote the interests of the poor but even so it is usually, although not exclusively, best achieved by stressing how reform meets the needs of the majority. See the Child Benefit campaign described in Frank Field, *Politics and Poverty*, Heinemann, 1982.

31. There are two background publications for this lecture: Frank Field and Matthew Owen, *Beyond Punishment – Hard Choices on the Road to Full Employability*; Frank Field, 1994, *How to Pay for the Future: Building a Stakeholders' Welfare*, 1996; Institute of Community Studies.

32 Brian Abel-Smith and Kay Titmuss, *The Philosophy of Welfare: Selected Writings of Richard M. Titmuss*, Allen & Unwin, 1987.

33 Samuel Smiles, *Self-help*, 1859, John Murray. Republished 1996, Institute of Economic Affairs.

34 There are two background publications for this lecture: Frank Field, *How to Pay for the Future: Building a Stakeholders' Welfare*, 1995; Frank Field, *Making Welfare Work*, 1995; Institute of Community Studies.

35 Nicholas Bosanquet, *Public Spending into the Millennium*, Social Market Foundation, 1995.

36 There are two background publications for this lecture: Frank Field, *How to Pay for the Future: Building a Stakeholders' Welfare*, 1995; Frank Field, *Making Welfare Work*, 1995; Institute of Community Studies.

Papers in Print

11. Standards in Schools: Assessment, Accountability and the Purposes of Education
John Marks
£6.00

12. Deeper Share Ownership
Matthew Gaved, Anthony Goodman
£6.00

13. Fighting Leviathan: Building Social Markets that Work
Howard Davies
£6.00

14. The Age of Entitlement
David Willetts
£6.00

15. Schools and the State
Evan Davis
£6.00

16. Public Sector Pay: In Search of Sanity
Ron Beadle
£8.00

17. Beyond Next Steps: a Civil Service for the 1990s
Sir Peter Kemp
£8.00

18. Post-Communist Societies in Transition: A Social Market Perspective
John Gray
£8.00

19. Two Cheers for the Institutions
Stanley Wright
£10.00

20. Civic Conservatism
David Willetts
£10.00

21. The Undoing of Conservatism
John Gray
£10.00

22. Meritocracy and the 'Classless Society'
    Adrian Wooldridge
    £12.00

23. Public Spending into the Millennium
    Nick Bosanquet
    £10.00

24. Communities in the Countryside
    Damian Green
    £10.00

25. The Ties that Bind Us
    Matthew d'Ancona
    £10.00

26. The Prospects for Public Spending
    Andrew Tyrie
    £15.00

27. Taxing and Spending Dilemmas
    Norman Gemmell
    £10.00

28. Making Shoplifters Pay: Retail Civil Recovery
    Joshua Bamfield
    £12.00

29. Britain's Relative Economic Decline 1870–1995: A Quantitative Perspective
    Nicholas Crafts
    £12.00

30. Beyond the Welfare State
    Robert Skidelsky
    £12.00

31. Lessons from the Republicans
    Tim Hames and Alan Grant
    £12.00

32. Reforming Welfare
    Frank Field
    £10.00

Reports

1. Environment, Economics and Development after the 'Earth Summit'
   Andrew Cooper
   £3.00

2. Another Great Depression? Historical Lessons for the 1990s
   Robert Skidelsky, Liam Halligan
   £5.00

3. Exiting the Underclass: Policy towards America's Urban Poor
   Andrew Cooper, Catherine Moylan
   £5.00

4. Britain's Borrowing Problem
   Bill Robinson
   £5.00

Occasional Papers

1. Deregulation
   David Willetts
   £3.00

2. 'There is No Such Thing as Society'
   Samuel Brittan
   £3.00

3. The Opportunities for Private Funding in the NHS
   David Willetts
   £3.00

4. A Social Market for Training
   Howard Davies
   £3.00

5. Beyond Unemployment
   Robert Skidelsky, Liam Halligan
   £6.00

6. Brighter Schools
   Michael Fallon
   £6.00

7. Understanding 'Shock Therapy'
   Jeffrey Sachs
   £8.00

8. Recruiting to the Little Platoons
   William Waldegrave   •
   £6.00

9. The Culture of Anxiety: The Middle Class in Crisis
   Matthew Symonds
   £8.00

10. What is left of Keynes?
    Samuel Brittan, Meghnad Desai, Deepak Lal, Robert Skidelsky, Tom Wilson
    £8.00

11. Winning the Welfare Debate
    Peter Lilley (Introduction by Frank Field)
    £10.00

12. Financing the Future of the Welfare State
    Robert Skidelsky, Will Hutton
    £8.00

13. Picking Winners: The East Asian Experience
    Ian Little
    £8.00

14. Over-the-Counter Medicines
    Alan Maynard, Gerald Richardson
    £10.00

15. Pressure Group Politics in Modern Britain
    Riddell, Waldegrave, Secrett, Bazalgette, Gaines, Parminter
    £10.00

16. Design Decisions: Improving the Public Effectiveness of Public Purchasing
    Taylor, Fisher, Sorrell, Stephenson, Rawsthorn, Davis, Jenkins, Turner, Taylor
    £10.00

17. Stakeholder Society vs Enterprise Centre of Europe
    Robert Skidelsky, Will Hutton
    £10.00

18. Setting Enterprise Free
    Ian Lang
    £10.00

19. Community Values and the Market Economy
    John Kay
    £10.00

Other Papers

Local Government and the Social Market
George Jones
£3.00

Full Employment without Inflation
James Meade
£6.00

Memoranda

1. Provider Choice: 'Opting In' through the Private Finance Initiative
   Michael Fallon
   £5.00

2. The Importance of Resource Accounting
   Evan Davis
   £3.50

3. Why There is No Time to Teach:
   What is wrong with the National Curriculum 10 Level Scale
   John Marks
   £5.00

4. All Free Health Care Must be Effective
   Brendan Devlin, Gwyn Bevan
   £5.00

5. Recruiting to the Little Platoons
   William Waldegrave

   £5.00

6. Labour and the Public Services
   John Willman
   £8.00

7. Organising Cost Effective Access to Justice
    Gwyn Bevan, Tony Holland and Michael Partington
    £5.00

8. A Memo to Modernisers
    Ron Beadle, Andrew Cooper, Evan Davis, Alex de Mont,
    Stephen Pollard, David Sainsbury, John Willman
    £8.00

9. Conservatives in Opposition: Republicans in the US
    Daniel Finkelstein
    £5.00

10. Housing Benefit: Incentives for Reform
    Greg Clark
    £8.00

11. The Market and Clause IV
    Stephen Pollard
    £5.00

12. Yeltsin's Choice: Background to the Chechnya Crisis
    Vladimir Mau
    £8.00

13. Teachers' Practices: A New Model for State Schools
    Tony Meredith
    £8.00

14. The Right to Earn: Learning to Live with Top People's Pay
    Ron Beadle
    £8.00

15. A Memo to Modernisers II
    John Abbott, Peter Boone, Tom Chandos, Evan Davis, Alex de Mont, Ian Pearson MP,
    Stephen Pollard, Katharine Raymond, John Spiers
    £8.00

16. Schools, Selection and the Left
    Stephen Pollard
    £8.00

17. The Future of Long-Term Care
    Andrew Cooper, Roderick Nye
    £8.00

Trident Trust / SMF Contributions to Policy

Hard Data

1. The Rowntree Inquiry and 'Trickle Down'
   Andrew Cooper, Roderick Nye
   £5.00

2. Costing the Public Policy Agenda: A week of the *Today* Programme
   Andrew Cooper
   £5.00

3. Universal Nursery Education and Playgroups
   Andrew Cooper, Roderick Nye
   £5.00

4. Social Security Costs of the Social Chapter
   Andrew Cooper, Marc Shaw
   £5.00

5. What Price a Life?
   Andrew Cooper, Roderick Nye
   £5.00

Centre for Post-Collectivist Studies

1. Russia's Stormy Path to Reform
   Robert Skidelsky (ed.)
   £20.00

2. Macroeconomic Stabilisation in Russia: Lessons of Reforms, 1992–1995
   Robert Skidelsky, Liam Halligan
   £10.00

3. The End of Order
   Francis Fukuyama
   £9.50

Briefings

1. A Guide to Russia's Parliamentary Elections
   Liam Halligan, Boris Mozdoukhov
   £10.00